Canon®
Speedlite System
Digital Field Guide

Canon®
Speedlite System
Digital Field Guide

J. Dennis Thomas

Wiley Publishing, Inc.

Canon® Speedlite System Digital Field Guide

Published by
Wiley Publishing, Inc.
111 River Street
Hoboken, N.J. 07030-5774
www.wiley.com

Copyright © 2007 by Wiley Publishing, Inc., Indianapolis, Indiana

Published simultaneously in Canada

Library of Congress Control Number: 2006939436

ISBN: 978-0-470-04528-2

Manufactured in the United States of America

10 9 8 7 6 5 4 3 2 1

WILEY

About the Author

J. Dennis Thomas, known to his friends as Denny, has been interested in photography since his early teens when he found some of his father's old photography equipment and photographs of the Vietnam War. Fortunately, he was able to take photography classes with an amazing teacher that started him on a path of learning that has never stopped.

Denny's first paying photography gig was in 1990 when he was asked to do promotional shots for a band being promoted by Warner Bros. Records. Although he has pursued many different career paths through the years, including a few years of being a musician, his love of photography and the printed image has never waned.

With the advent of digital photography, although he was resistant to give up film, Denny realized there was yet more to learn in the realm of photography. It was just like starting all over. Photography was fresh and exciting again. Realizing that the world of digital photography was complex and new, Denny decided to pursue a degree in photography in order to learn the complex techniques of digital imaging with the utmost proficiency.

Eventually Denny decided to turn his life-long passion into a full-time job. Denny currently owns his own company, Dead Sailor Productions, a photography and graphic design business. He does freelance work for companies including RedBull Energy Drink, Obsolete Industries, Secret Hideout Studios, and Digital Race Photography. He still continues to photograph bands, including LA Guns, the US Bombs, Skid Row, Quiet Riot, Echo & the Bunnymen, Dick Dale, Link Wray, Willie Nelson, Bo Diddley, and the Rolling Stones. He has been published in several regional publications and continues to show his work in various galleries throughout the country.

Credits

Project Editor
Cricket Krengel

Technical Editor
Michael Guncheon

Copy Editor
Jerelind Charles

Product Development Supervisor
Courtney Allen

Editorial Manager
Robyn B. Siesky

Vice President & Group Executive Publisher
Richard Swadley

Vice President & Publisher
Barry Pruett

Business Manager
Amy Knies

Project Coordinator
Adrienne Martinez

Graphics and Production Specialists
Laura Campbell
Shawn Frazier
Shane Johnson
Jennifer Mayberry
Ronald Terry

Quality Control Technicians
Laura Albert
Dwight Ramsey

Proofreading
ConText Editorial Services, Inc.

Indexing
Valerie Haynes Perry

Wiley Bicentennial Logo
Richard J. Pacifico

This book is dedicated to my family.

To Hunter and Dylan, Mom, Dad, Diana, Tami, and the rest...

Acknowledgments

Thanks to Jack Puryear at Puryear Digital Photography, the faculty and staff at Austin Community College, all the bands and models, and Cricket and Courtney at Wiley Publishing.

Contents at a Glance

Contents

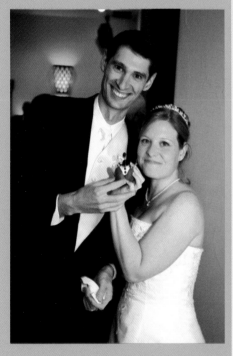

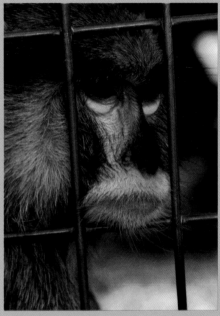

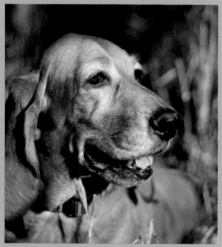

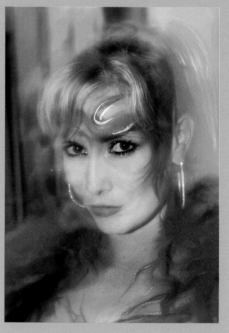

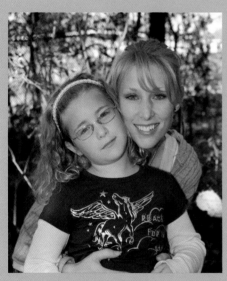

Chapter 5: Setting Up a Wireless Studio 77

Chapter 6: Real-World Applications 95

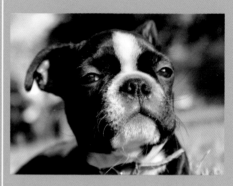

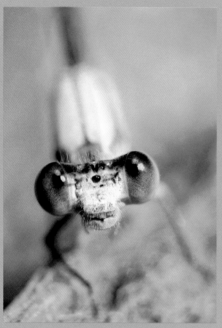

Chapter 7: Simple Posing for Great Portraits 161

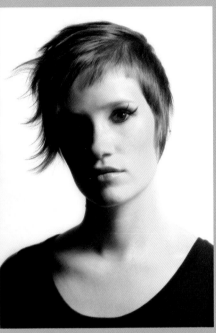

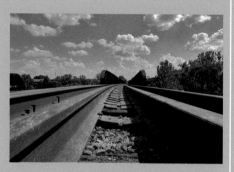
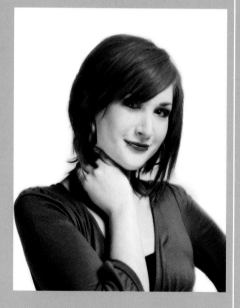
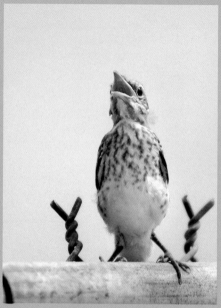

Introduction

For the most part, traditional flash photography has been a mystifying undertaking for a lot of amateur photographers. You had to learn all sorts of arcane terms and equations in order to get the right exposure. Then when you succeeded in getting the exposure right it just didn't look natural.

With Canon's Speedlite System, much of the worry and confusion has been removed! A Canon Speedlite is able to do the exposure calculations for you, along with balancing the flash exposure with the ambient lighting allowing for a more natural look.

But using a flash isn't all there is to taking great flash photographs. The next step in this process is learning about the subtleties of lighting. It's about light placement and modifying the lights for different and creative looks. It's about going beyond the everyday flash snapshot and creating truly dazzling images.

This book helps you to better understand and use the Canon Speedlite System to get the excellent flash photos you know you can take.

A Little History of Canon's Speedlite System

The first Canon Speedlite that offered any type of automatic flash was the 300TL, introduced about 1986, which was designed to be used with the Canon T90 film camera. The A-TTL (advanced-through-the-lens) auto flash system was a great advance considering before this all calculations had to be done by hand: measuring the distance from the flash to the subject, figuring out the flash power, and deciding how much power to use for the aperture that was required for the shot.

A-TTL was Canon's advancement on standard TTL auto flash. Basically, how standard TTL auto flash works is, a sensor in the camera measures the light reflected off of the film plane. When the sensor determines there is enough light to sufficiently expose a neutral subject, the flash cuts off. Although TTL was better than manually setting the flash, it was far from ideal. Canon set out to improve this when it introduced A-TTL.

Canon's A-TTL, available with the 300TL and subsequently on the EZ model Speedlites, fires a pre-flash before the actual exposure while the camera is metering, determining the proper flash exposure while retaining readings for the ambient light. The camera then uses both of these readings to provide a natural-looking picture by using the ambient light for the main exposure and light from the Speedlite as a fill-flash. This is known in Canon's nomenclature as "auto-fill reduction." When the camera meter determines that there is not enough ambient light for proper exposure, the flash is then used as the main light for the subject's exposure.

Although A-TTL seemed like a good thing, it has many design flaws and drawbacks. Some of these drawbacks include using a sensor on the flash to determine the light output instead of using a sensor in the camera and having the pre-flash fire when the shutter was half-depressed. It also isn't very useful when trying to bounce flash.

In 1995 Canon introduced E-TTL or "evaluative through-the-lens" flash metering. The advancement on A-TTL is that E-TTL fires a low-power pre-flash immediately before the shutter opens, rather than when the shutter is half-depressed.

Canon's E-TTL metering system also improves on A-TTL by providing a more subtle and natural looking fill flash when used in a daylight situation. It does this by partly basing the exposure on the autofocus point that is locked onto the subject rather than using multiple zones as it had done in the past.

In 2004, with the advent of the EOS 1D mkII, Canon introduced E-TTL II. This is very similar to the original E-TTL with a couple of small improvements. The first improvement Canon made is in the way the E-TTL II meters the light. With E-TTL II, the camera takes a reading of the scene both before and after the pre-flash fires to help reduce false readings that can be caused by any reflective substances in the scene. Secondly, Canon added the ability to use distance information supplied by certain lenses to help obtain the correct flash exposure.

What's in This Book for You?

While the manuals that come with the Speedlites are informative and contain all the technical data about your Canon Speedlite, they don't exactly go into detail about the nuances of lighting — the nuances and pitfalls you may encounter or the types of settings you might want to use on your camera and lenses when working with your Speedlites.

That's where this book comes in. This book offers you tips and advice based on real-world experiences of a photographer who has been using the Canon Speedlite System.

Initially, flash photography is often thought of with dread as mysterious and confusing. However, with this book, I hope to dispel that myth and help to get you on the road to using the flash as another creative tool in your photographic arsenal, rather than something to be avoided at all costs.

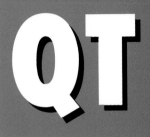

Quick Tour

✦　　✦　　✦　　✦

In This Chapter

Getting up and running quickly

Taking your first photos with the Speedlite

✦　　✦　　✦　　✦

Many cameras come equipped with a built-in flash. Like any photographer who takes many photos with flash, you soon learn the limitations of these built-in flashes. In order to obtain better flash lighting for portraits, still life photos, and other types of photography, the next step is to graduate to external Speedlites, such as the Canon 580 EX or 430EX. By adding Speedlites to your photographic arsenal, you get many further-reaching photographic capabilities your built-in flash just can't provide.

Though many would think that advanced flash units such as the 580EX or 430EX are complex accessories, the reality is, they are ready-to-go for quick snapshots, but also configurable for some complex wireless multi-flash photo shoots. So get ready, you are about to explore the world of the 580EX and 430EX Speedlites and the Canon Speedlite system.

This quick tour shows you how to get up and going with your 580EX or 430EX Speedlite to take great flash photos immediately.

Getting Up and Running Quickly

If you want to start using your new Canon 580EX or 430EX Speedlite right away, all you really need to do is insert the batteries, attach the Speedlite to your camera's hot shoe, and then turn both the Speedlite and the camera on. You'll be amazed at the quality of flash photos you can take with the Speedlite as soon as you take it out of the box.

 Note *The flash accepts Alkaline, Lithium, or rechargeable AA-sized batteries.*

To attach the Speedlite:

1. **Turn off the camera and Speedlite.** Both the Speedlite and camera should be turned off before attaching. Turning off the equipment reduces any risk of short-circuits when attaching different electronic devices.

2. **Unlock the mounting foot locking wheel.** Turn the mounting foot locking wheel of the Speedlite to the right — its unlocked position.

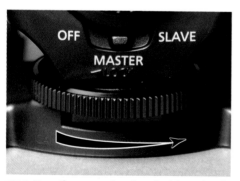

QT.1 Turn the mounting foot locking wheel to the right to unlock.

3. **Attach the Speedlite to your camera.** Slide the Speedlite hot shoe into the camera's hot shoe. Turn the mounting foot locking wheel to the left to lock the Speedlite into place.

4. **Position the flash head to the horizontal position.** When you first attach the Speedlite to your camera, make sure the flash head is positioned in its normal horizontal position. You can reposition the flash head by pressing the flash head tilting/rotating lock release, and then positioning the flash head.

 Note *When using the 580EX, if the flash head is not in the normal, horizontal position, the LCD panel shows a warning.*

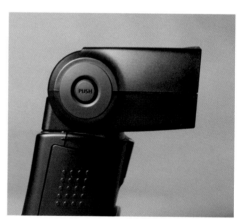

QT.2 Position the flash head in the horizontal position by pressing the flash head tilting/rotating lock release, shown here highlighted in green.

5. **Turn on your camera.**

6. **Turn on your Speedlite.** The On/Off switch for the Speedlite is located on the back panel, shown in Figure QT.3.

After you power up your Speedlite and camera with the flash head in the horizontal position, both the flash and camera sync. You can then reposition the flash head to your desired position.

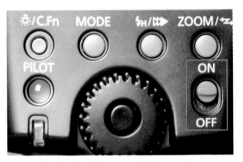

QT.3 The back of the 580EX Speedlite

Taking Your First Photos with the Speedlite

After you get your flash attached and turned on, the flash default sets itself to E-TTL mode. *E-TTL* stands for Evaluative Through the Lens, which means that the light meter in the camera takes a reading through the lens and decides how much flash exposure you need depending on your camera settings.

Depending on which metering pattern your camera is set to, the flash will either add fill flash or expose for the subject only.

✦ If your camera meter is set to evaluative metering, which means the light meter is taking a reading of the whole scene, the camera adjusts the flash exposure to match the ambient light, adding fill flash to create a more natural look.

✦ If your camera is set to spot meter the scene, the flash sets to full TTL mode. The camera's meter takes a reading of the subject and exposes just for that, not taking into account the background light.

I recommend setting your camera to evaluative metering mode and using the E-TTL mode when you are just getting started. This mode produces great results, and you don't have to do anything but press the shutter release. When set to spot metering and E-TTL, the background tends to be too dark or the subject seems to be unnaturally bright.

Tip *Don't be afraid to use your flash outside with sun. This is where E-TTL fill flash excels. The flash fills in some of the harsh shadows than are created by the sun.*

Taking photos with the Speedlite on TTL is just as easy as taking photos without a flash. Just press the shutter release. The camera makes all of the adjustments for exposure and adjusts the *flash head zoom* for you.

The flash head zoom is a feature of the Speedlite that adjusts the flash to match the focal length of the lens you're using. Don't be concerned if you don't completely understand how E-TTL flash works or why the flash zoom is important—you will in good time. By the time you finish this book, you should be an expert. In the meantime, this Quick Tour is just to get you started with flash photography and comfortable with your new flash equipment.

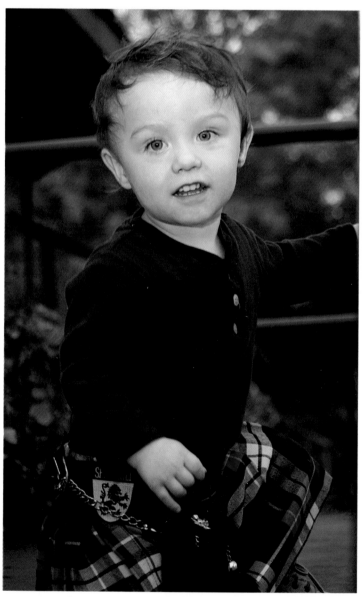

QT.4 An outdoor portrait using E-TTL with evaluative metering.

Everything is attached and you have the basic settings, so get out there and shoot. Take some pictures of your friends or significant other. Get your dog or cat posed. Set up a still life. Experiment with different apertures and shutter speeds. Above all, have fun!

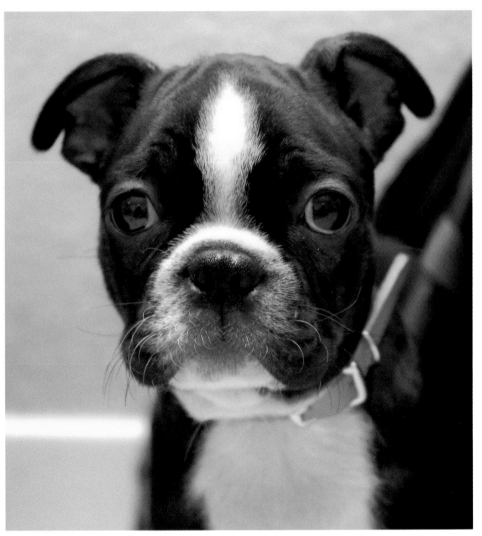

QT.5 A quick snapshot of Henrietta taken using the 430EX with a wide aperture

Using Canon Speedlites

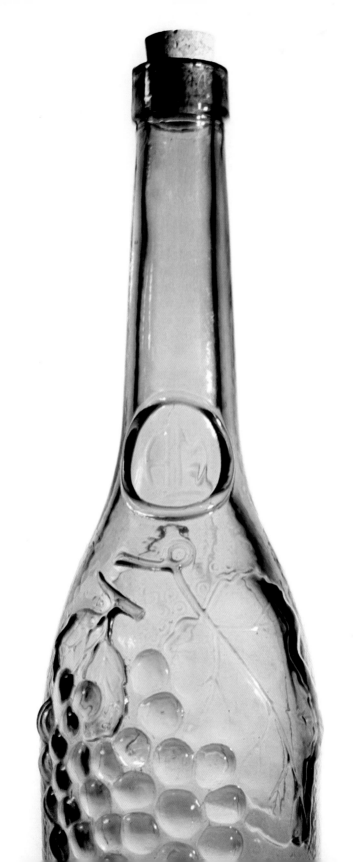

Exploring the 580EX and 430EX

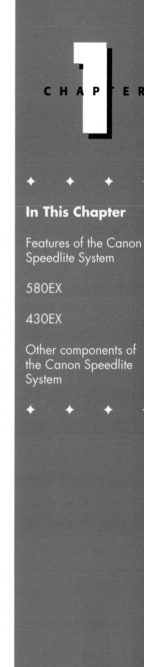

As with any new camera equipment, it is important to know how everything works and where all the controls are. So, in this chapter you take a look at the main features and functions of the major components in the Canon Speedlite System, including the 580EX and the 430EX. Additionally, this chapter also touches on some features and functions of the ST-E2 wireless commander and the MT-24EX macro Speedlite kit. By the end of the chapter, you ought to have an in-depth knowledge of what all the buttons do and how they function with your Speedlite.

Features of the Canon Speedlite System

The components of the Canon Speedlite System are any Canon dSLR and the 580EX, 430EX Speedlites. Additional components include the ST-E2 commander unit, and the MT-24EX macro lighting kit. All Canon EOS dSLRs can be used with the Canon Speedlite system, and all features are available with every camera.

In this section you also look at all of the available features of the Canon Speedlite System.

✦ **E-TTL II.** Canon's most advanced metering system, this metering system uses preflashes and flash metering algorithms to determine the proper flash exposure. The E-TTL II system reads information from all metering zones before and after the preflash. Areas with little change in brightness are then weighted for flash metering. This is done to avoid a highly reflective surface from creating a false reading thereby causing under-exposure. When using certain EF lenses, distance information is also entered into the equation.

✦ **Flash Exposure Lock (FEL).** The FEL enables you to meter the subject, getting a reading for the proper flash exposure. Pressing the FEL button enables you to meter the subject and then recompose the shot while maintaining the proper flash exposure for the subject.

> **Note** Some camera bodies have a separate FEL button, while some have a button that can be assigned to FEL function.

✦ **Wireless Lighting.** This feature enables you to use your Speedlites wirelessly. The master unit fires preflashes, which transmits information back and forth between the camera and the flash. When using this feature you need to have either a 580EX or an ST-E2 wireless transmitter as a *master unit*. The master unit can control multiple Speedlites wirelessly, allowing more creative lighting possibilities.

✦ **High-Speed Sync.** This feature allows you to use your flash at higher shutter speed than your camera body is rated for. You may want to use this feature when shooting outdoor portraits requiring a wide aperture and high shutter speed.

✦ **AF-Assist beam.** The 580EX and 430EX have a built-in LED that emits a light pattern to give the camera's autofocus (AF) something to lock onto.

✦ **Flash Color Information Communication.** As the flash duration gets longer, the color temperature changes a bit. The 580EX and 430EX transmit this change to the camera body ensuring a more accurate white balance.

580EX

The 580EX has many great features and offers a great deal of versatility when shooting with flash. As you no doubt already have the flash and have read the manual (or at least skimmed through it), you should know the basics about your Speedlite already. But, before you go much further, you should familiarize yourself with the Speedlite.

580EX specs and features

This section provides a brief look at different features that are available on the 580EX Speedlite.

✦ **Guide Number.** 118 at ISO 100 on the 35mm setting. See your owner's manual for more specifics on GNs for specific zoom ranges.

Understanding the Guide Number

Although the actual power of the flash is fixed, the Guide Number (GN) of the flash changes with the ISO setting of the camera and also varies with the zoom setting of the flash. This is due to the increased sensitivity of the sensor and the actual dispersion of the light when set to a specific zoom range. When the ISO is at a higher setting, the sensor is more sensitive to light, in effect making the flash more powerful, hence a higher GN.

Also, when the zoom is set to a wide-angle, the flash tube is set further back in the flash head, diffusing the light and giving it wider coverage. This makes the flash somewhat less bright, thereby warranting a lower GN.

Remember that the Guide Number is exactly that — a guide. In reality, it is nothing more than a number assigned by the manufacturer to assist you in obtaining the correct exposure (and also a means of comparing light output among different Speedlites). Refer to your owner's manual for a table with the GN of the Speedlite at the specific zoom ranges.

✦ **Automatic zooming flash head.** Provides lens coverage from 24mm up to 105mm. 14mm with the included wide-angle adaptor.

✦ **E-TTL.** Supports E-TTL II, E-TTL, and full Manual operation.

✦ **Wireless Lighting.** This enables you to control up to three different groups of Speedlites in E-TTL or M mode.

✦ **Slow Sync.** Enables you to match the ambient background lighting with the flash so the background doesn't end up black.

✦ **Second Curtain Sync.** This function fires the flash at the end of the exposure as opposed to at the beginning of the exposure. This helps with more natural images when shooting long exposures, as it causes a trail to be behind a moving subject and not in front of it as occurs when the flash is fired at the beginning of the exposure.

✦ **Red-eye reduction.** Fires off a pre-flash to contract the pupils to avoid that eerie red glow.

✦ **AF-Assist beam.** Emits an array of light from an LED to assist in focusing in low-light situations.

✦ **High-Speed Sync (FP flash).** This function allows you to shoot with a shutter speed higher than the rated sync speed of the camera. This feature is useful when shooting portraits in bright light using a wide aperture to blur the background.

✦ **Flash Exposure Lock (FEL).** Using the FEL lock, you can get a reading from your subject and then recompose the shot while retaining the original exposure.

✦ **Modeling flash.** Releases short burst of flashes allowing you to see what the light falling on your subject looks like.

✦ **Multi Stroboscopic Flash mode.** Fires off a specific amount of flashes like a strobe light.

✦ **Tilting/rotating flash head for bouncing flash.** Allows you to point the flash head up for bouncing light from the ceiling or to the side to bounce off of the wall. The 580EX also allows you to tilt the head downward -7° for close-up subjects.

Main parts

The main parts of the 580EX Speedlite are identified and discussed in the following sections. Figures and explanations of each part and feature are included so that you have a clear understanding of how each is used.

✦ **Flash head.** This is where the flashbulb is located. Inside is a mechanism that zooms the flashbulb back and forth to provide flash coverage for lenses of different focal lengths. The flash head is adjustable; it can be tilted upward to 90° and downward to -7°. It can also be adjusted horizontally 180° to the left or to the right.

✦ **Flash head lock release button.** This button releases the flash head lock allowing you to adjust the angle for bounce flash.

✦ **Battery compartment lid.** Slide this downward to open the battery compartment to change out the batteries.

✦ **Light sensor for E-TTL wireless flash.** This sensor reads signals from Master unit enabling wireless flash.

✦ **AF-assist beam.** Emits a LED light array to achieve focus in low-light situations.

✦ **Wireless remote ready light.** This works as a ready light when the Speedlite is being used as a remote flash.

✦ **Flash head tilting angle scale.** Allows you to set the flash head at 45°, 60°, 75°, or 90° tilt.

✦ **LCD panel.** This panel is where you view all of the Speedlite settings and controls.

✦ **Control buttons.** Use these buttons to set and change settings on the Speedlite.

✦ **Pilot light.** Lights up indicating the Speedlite is ready to fire. After the Speedlite is fired, this light blinks until the Speedlite is fully recycled and ready to fire again.

✦ **Master/Slave setting switch.** Used to switch between using the 580EX as a master, a slave, or in the off position, as an on camera flash.

✦ **Mounting foot locking wheel.** Locks the Speedlite into the hot shoe or the Speedlite stand.

✦ **Wide-angle lens adaptor.** This built-in diffuser provides you with the ability to use the Speedlite with a lens as wide as 14mm without having light fall-off at the edges of the image.

✦ **Bounce or catchlight card.** This white card reflects light down into the eyes providing a catchlight when the flash is used in the bounced position.

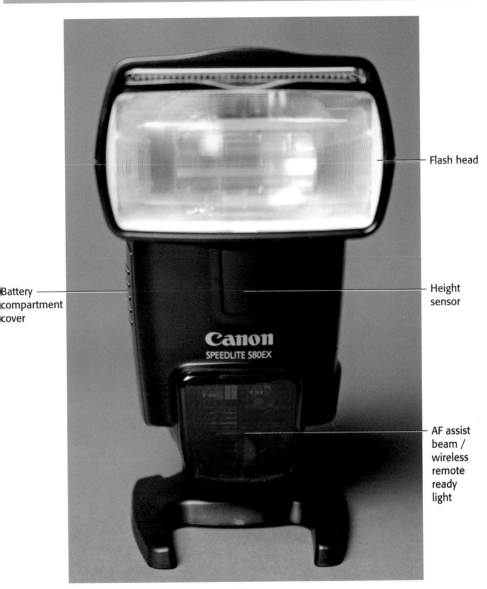

Flash head

Battery
compartment
cover

Height
sensor

AF assist
beam /
wireless
remote
ready
light

1.1 The front of the 580EX Speedlite

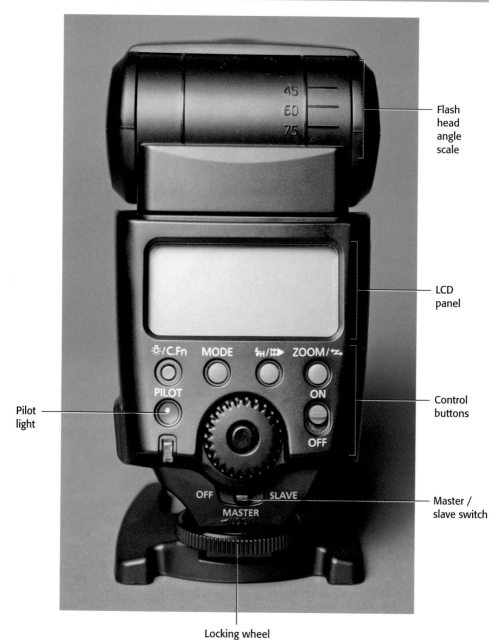

Flash
head
angle
scale

LCD
panel

Control
buttons

Pilot
light

Master /
slave switch

Locking wheel

1.2 The back of the 580EX Speedlite

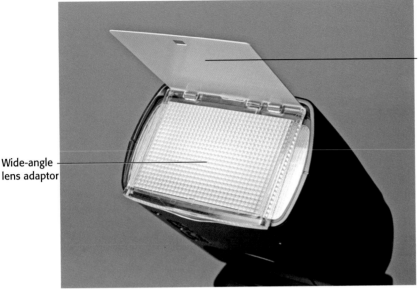

Bounce / catchlight card

Wide-angle lens adaptor

1.3 Wide-angle lens adaptor and built-in catchlight card

✦ **External power source terminal.** Canon's optional external power source can be plugged in to this terminal. This power supply is called the Compact Battery Pack CP-E3.

✦ **Speedlite bracket fitting.** This is used to attach the Speedlite to the Canon SB-E1 Speedlite Bracket. The SB-E1 allows the Speedlite to be attached to the side of the camera rather than to the hot shoe.

✦ **Hot shoe mounting foot.** This slides into the hot shoe on your camera body and locks down with the locking wheel.

✦ **Flash head rotating angle scale.** This enables you to rotate the flash head horizontally left 60°, 75°, 90°, 120°, 150°, and 180°. To the right it can be adjusted 60°, 75°, 90°, 120°, 150°, and 180°.

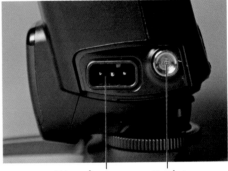

External power source terminal   Bracket fitting

1.4 External power supply terminal (left) and Speedlite bracket fitting (right)

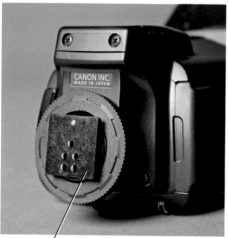

Hot shoe
mounting foot

1.5 The hot shoe mounting foot

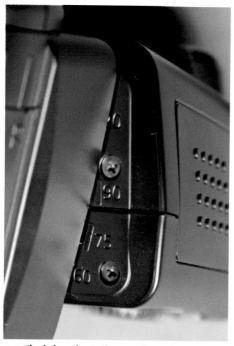

1.6 Flash head rotating angle scale

Control buttons

There are several control buttons on the 580EX, and you should know what each of them does in order to get the best results from your Speedlite. Some of them are obvious, such as the On/Off switch, but others control the menus you select. You need to know how to navigate your Speedlite.

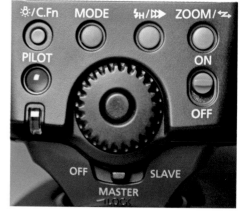

1.7 580EX control panel

✦ **Select dial and the Select/Set button.** You can scroll the main button left or right and press the center button.

  • **Left and right.** When scrolled left or right, you use this button to change the zoom of the flash, flash exposure compensation, or flash bracketing settings.

  • **Select.** The center button is the Select/Set button. This button is used to select the flash exposure compensation settings. Pressing it a second time selects the settings for flash bracketing.

✦ **On/Off switch.** This button does just what it says it does. Slide it up or down to turn the Speedlite on or off.

✦ **Pilot Light button.** Press this lighted button to test fire the 580EX to ensure it is functioning properly or to take a test reading using a handheld flash meter. This button also lets you know when the flash is fully charged and ready to fire. When the light is red, the flash is ready to fire at full power.

✦ **Mode button.** The Mode button is used to cycle through the LCD menu among the different flash modes of the 580EX Speedlite. The different modes are:

- **E-TTL.** The exposure is determined by the camera and matched with the ambient light.

- **M (full Manual mode).** You determine the flash power by using the Guide Number of the flash and dividing this number by the distance of the Speedlite from the subject, with the quotient being the aperture to which you need to set your camera. You can also use a flash meter to determine the flash and camera settings.

- **Multi Stroboscopic Flash.** This mode allows you to fire the flash multiple times for a single exposure.

✦ **LCD light/C.fn button.** Pressing this button once turns the LCD light on for viewing in dim light. Pressing and holding this button brings you to the Custom functions menu. The custom functions are set using the select dial.

✦ **High Speed sync/FEB button.** Pressing this button once allows you to set the flash to High Speed Sync. Pressing it a second time turns on the Flash Exposure Bracketing feature.

✦ **Zoom button.** Allows you to manually change the flash head zoom using the control dial.

580EX accessories

Along with the SS-800 soft case for storing and carrying your 580EX, it also includes a Speedlite stand that enables you to mount your 580EX to a stand or tripod, which also makes it easier to balance the Speedlite on a flat surface.

430EX

The 430EX, while not as feature-rich as the 580EX, still has most of the features that you will find useful when shooting with flash. As with the 580EX, you likely have the flash in hand and have at least skimmed through the manual. At this point, you are probably familiar with the basic features of your Speedlite. The material in the next few sections gives you a better idea of not only what the features are, but also why they are important.

430EX feature overview

The 430EX has fewer features and a lower Guide Number than the 580EX, but it's still a great flash. Most of the missing features are shooting modes that you may find aren't necessary to have. And, although the GN is lower, the 430EX is still a powerful flash. Firing the 430EX at full power using an aperture of f/2.8, it's possible to get a fairly well-lit shot at almost 200 feet.

This section provides a brief look at different features that are available on the 430EX Speedlite. It is important to note, however, that some features may not be available to use depending on the camera body you are using.

✦ **Guide Number.** 101.7 at ISO 100 on the 35mm setting. See your owner's manual for more specifics on GNs for specific zoom ranges.

✦ **Automatic zooming flash head.** Provides lens coverage from 24mm up to 105mm. 14mm with the included wide-angle adaptor.

✦ **E-TTL.** Supports E-TTL II, E-TTL, TTL, and full Manual operation.

✦ **Slow Sync.** Enables you to match the ambient background lighting with the flash so the background doesn't end up black.

✦ **Red-eye reduction.** Fires off a pre-flash to contract the pupils to avoid red glowing eyes.

✦ **AF-Assist beam.** Emits an array of light from an LED to assist in focusing in low-light situations.

✦ **High-Speed Sync.** Allows you to shoot with a shutter speed higher than the rated sync speed of the camera. This is useful when shooting portraits in bright light using a wide aperture to blur the background.

✦ **Modeling flash.** Releases a short burst of flashes allowing you to see what the light falling on your subject looks like.

✦ **Tilting/rotating flash-head for bouncing flash.** Allows you to point the flash head up for bouncing light from the ceiling or to the side to bounce off of the wall.

Main parts

Even though the 430EX Speedlite is similar to the 580EX, it is still important to go over each of the important parts of the equipment. I include figures and explanations of the parts and features to give you a better understanding of how each is used.

✦ **Flash head.** This is where the flashbulb is located. Inside is a mechanism that zooms the flashbulb back and forth to provide flash coverage for lenses of different focal lengths. The flash head is adjustable; it can be tilted upward to 90°. It can also be adjusted horizontally 180° to the left or 90° to the right.

✦ **Flash head lock release button.** This button releases the flash head lock allowing you to adjust the angle for bounce flash.

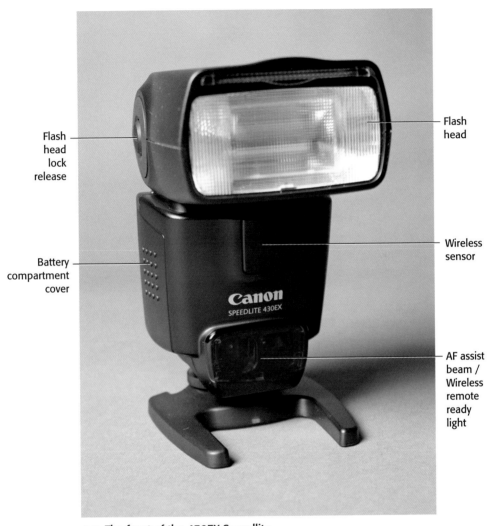

Flash head lock release

Battery compartment cover

Flash head

Wireless sensor

AF assist beam / Wireless remote ready light

1.8 The front of the 430EX Speedlite

✦ **Battery compartment cover.** Slide this downward to open the battery compartment to change out the batteries.

✦ **Light sensor for TTL wireless flash.** This sensor reads signals from Commander units enabling wireless flash.

✦ **Wireless remote ready light.** This works as a ready light when the 430EX is being used as a remote flash.

✦ **AF-assist illuminator.** Emits an LED light array to achieve focus in low-light situations.

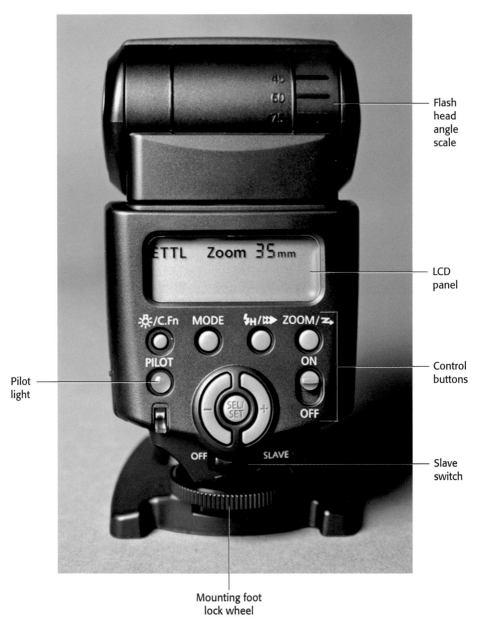

Flash head angle scale

LCD panel

Control buttons

Pilot light

Slave switch

Mounting foot lock wheel

1.9 The back of the 430EX Speedlite

✦ **Flash head tilting angle scale.**
Allows you to set the flash head at
45°, 60°, 75°, or 90° tilt.

✦ **LCD panel.** Where you view all the
Speedlite settings and controls.

✦ **Pilot light button.** This button lights up indicating that the Speedlite is ready to fire. After the Speedlite is fired, this light blinks until the Speedlite is fully recycled and ready to fire again. This button can also be pressed to test fire the Speedlite to check the output levels.

✦ **Control buttons.** Used to set and change settings on the Speedlite.

✦ **Mounting foot locking wheel.** Locks the Speedlite into the hot shoe or the Speedlite stand.

✦ **Slave mode selector switch.** Used to put the 430EX in slave mode.

✦ **Wide-angle lens adaptor.** This built-in diffuser provides you with the ability to use the Speedlite with a lens as wide as 14mm without having light fall-off at the edges of the image.

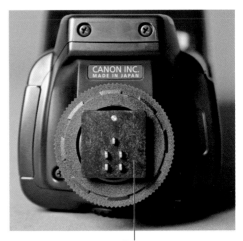

Hot shoe
mounting foot

1.11 Hot shoe mounting foot

✦ **Flash head rotating angle scale.** The Speedlite flash head can rotate horizontally left 60°, 75°, 90°, 120°, 150°, and 180°. To the right it can be adjusted 60°, 75° and 90°.

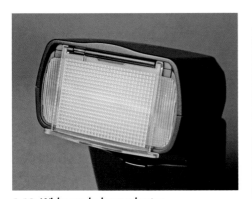

1.10 Wide-angle lens adaptor

✦ **Hot shoe mounting foot.** This slides into the hot shoe on your camera body and locks down with a lever.

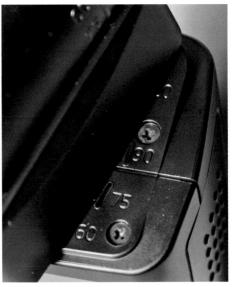

1.12 Flash head rotating angle scale

Control buttons

You should know what each of the various control buttons on the 430EX Speedlite can do to get the best results. The following sections describe them.

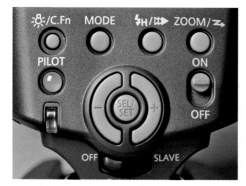

1.13 430EX control panel

✦ **On/Off switch.** Slide the switch up or down to turn the 430EX on or off.

✦ **Pilot light/button.** Press this button to test fire the 430EX to check for output. This button is lit red when the flash is fully charged and ready to fire at full power.

✦ **Zoom button.** Pressing this button enables you to change the zoom of the flash head to adjust for different focal length lenses using the +/- buttons. It allows coverage for 24mm to 105mm lenses. 14mm coverage is achieved with the built-in wide-angle diffuser.

✦ **LCD light/C.fn button.** Pressing this button once turns the LCD light on for viewing in dim light. Pressing and holding this button brings you to the Custom functions menu. The custom functions are set using the +/- buttons.

✦ **High Speed sync/FEB button.** Pressing this button once allows you to set the flash to High Speed sync. Pressing it a second time turns on the Flash Exposure Bracketing feature.

✦ **+/- buttons.** The +/- buttons are used to change the flash head zoom settings when in the zoom menu and they also allow you to change the custom functions settings when in the C.fn menu.

 Cross-Reference   *Chapter 2 covers the Custom Settings menu in more detail.*

✦ **Mode button.** The Mode button allows you to switch between the available flash modes. The modes available with the 430EX are:

• **E-TTL flash.** The exposure is determined by the camera and matched with the ambient light.

• **M (full Manual mode).** You determine the flash power.

430EX accessories

The Speedlite 430EX comes with a soft case for storage and carrying as well as the Speedlite stand, which not only allows you to mount your 430EX to a stand or tripod, but you can also use it to balance the Speedlite on a flat surface.

Other Components of the Speedlite System

You have your 580EX and 430EX Speedlites, but what else might you need to round out your Speedlite system? Just having one or both Speedlites is a great start, but that isn't all there is to the Canon Speedlite system.

ST-E2 wireless transmitter

A Master unit is what tells the remote Speedlites when to fire. It also reads the data provided by the remote Speedlites pre-flashes and relays the information to the camera body for use in setting the exposure levels.

The ST-E2 is an infrared wireless Master unit for the Canon Speedlite system. It functions in much the same way as the 580EX does in Master mode except that it doesn't emit any visible light. The ST-E2 Commander has four independent channels, so if you are working near other photographers, you can work on different channels so someone else's ST-E2 Commander won't set off your flashes.

The ST-E2 Transmitter slides into the hot shoe of your camera like any other Speedlite and is used to wirelessly control the 580EX, 430EX, or MT-24EX flashes. Each channel can be used to control two groups of flashes. From the ST-E2 you can control the output of each group individually. You can set each group to TTL or M in order to fine-tune the lighting to suit your needs.

MT-24EX Speedlite

The MT-24EX is a dedicated macro Speedlite. With macro flash photography, getting your flash on axis or on the same level as the subject is best. In macro photography, your lens is usually very close to your subject, which ends up blocking the light from an on-camera, shoe-mounted flash. This is where lens-mounted flashes come in.

The MT-24EX Speedlite has two separate flash heads that are attached to your lens by a mounting ring. The flash heads can attach to the ring and rotate or they can be removed from the ring for more control of the lighting placement. The MT-24 EX has a master unit that controls each flash head. The master unit is similar to the ST-E2 wireless transmitter and can also be used to fire external groups of Speedlites.

 Chapter 6 covers more macro lighting techniques.

MR-14EX ring lite

The MR-14EX ring lite is another type of Speedlite used for macro photography. It is very similar to the MT-24EX except that the flash heads can't be moved. Without being able to move the flash heads, the result of using this ring lite is often a very flat, even lighting that is common in most macro applications.

Like the ST-E2 and the MT-24EX the MR-14EX master unit can be used to trigger off-camera slave flashes such as the 580EX or the 430EX.

Setting Up the 580EX and 430EX

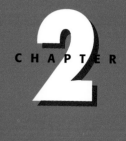
This chapter covers how to set up your Speedlites for various types of use. I discuss the different flash settings and offer suggestions on when to use them. You also learn how to set up your Speedlites for wireless use and how to set the zoom head for a specific lens.

Power Requirements

The power requirements for the 430EX and 580EX are the same: four AA-sized batteries. Having ample batteries for your Speedlite is very important. What's the use in having a wireless portable studio when your batteries die on you? You want to carry at least one extra set of batteries for each Speedlite you have.

If you're going to be using your Speedlites a lot, you may want to check into purchasing rechargeable batteries. The initial investment is a little more than standard alkaline batteries, but you make it back easily when you don't have to pay several dollars for batteries every couple of days when using the Speedlite frequently. I recommend buying two sets of rechargeable batteries for each Speedlite, which is worth it the long run. You don't want to have to stop in the middle of a shoot to run down to a convenience store to buy second-rate batteries for twice the normal price. Trust me, I've been there. I always have plenty of spare batteries with me now.

Five different types of AA batteries are available for use in Canon Speedlites that fall into two categories.

Non-rechargeable

If you are not ready to invest a set or two of rechargeable batteries for your Speedlites, you should consider your choices within the non-rechargeable variety before making additional battery purchases. The two types to choose from are

✦ **Alkaline-manganese.** These are your everyday, standard type of battery; alkaline batteries are available nearly everywhere from your local gas station to high-end camera shops. There can be differences in quality depending on the manufacturer. When buying these types of batteries, I suggest purchasing the batteries that specify they are for use with digital cameras. These batteries usually last longer than the cheaper brands.

✦ **Lithium.** Lithium batteries cost a little more than standard alkaline batteries, but they last a lot longer. You can find lithium batteries at specialty battery shops and some camera shops have them in stock.

Rechargeable

Rechargeable batteries do require more of an initial investment, but you easily get your money back in what you save by not having to buy disposable batteries often. The two types of rechargeable batteries to choose from for your Speedlites are

✦ **NiCd.** Nickel-cadmium batteries are the most common type of rechargeable batteries. You can find NiCd batteries pretty easily.

Department stores usually sell them along with a charger for under 20 dollars. Also, you can usually find them at most camera stores. While NiCd batteries are rechargeable, they don't last forever. After time they hold less and less of a charge until they're finally depleted. If the battery is repeatedly charged when it has not been fully exhausted, the life of the NiCd is even shorter. For example, if you come home from a shoot and your battery was only used to half of its capacity, you likely place it in the charger for your shoot tomorrow. After doing that a few times, the battery remembers that it only charges to half power, which is called battery memory. Some manufacturers, however, claim that battery memory does not exist.

✦ **Ni-MH.** Nickel–Metal Hydride batteries are the most expensive type of batteries, but as the saying goes, "you get what you pay for." AA Ni-MH batteries have two to three times the capacity of AA NiCd batteries, therefore they last longer on a single charge than NiCd batteries do, and the battery memory problem is not as significant. You can find Ni-MH batteries in specialty battery shops.

 Caution

With Ni-MH batteries, you must fully charge the batteries before you install them into your Speedlite. If one of the batteries in the set becomes discharged before the others, the discharged battery goes into polarity reversal, which means the positive and negative poles become reversed, causing permanent damage to the cells, rendering it useless and possibly damaging the Speedlite.

Canon also offers the CP-E3 battery pack which uses eight AA batteries, significantly reducing recycle time and doubling the working life of your Speedlite. Another option is the Canon Transistor Pack E, which holds six C-sized batteries for extra long battery life. For more information on these visit the Canon Web site.

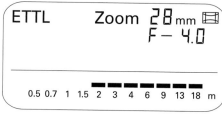

2.1 580EX LCD menu set to E-TTL

Flash Modes

The Canon Speedlites function with several different flash modes. These modes differ based on which model of Speedlite you're using. The 580EX has a couple of more options than the 430EX does. These different modes enable you to customize how your Speedlite reacts to your specific camera settings.

 Note Both Speedlites offer backward-compatible flash modes for use with pre–2004 Canon dSLRs and SLR film cameras.

E-TTL II

E-TTL II is the newest and most innovative flash mode by Canon. It was introduced in 2004 for use with the Canon EOS 1D mkII. Its use continues with all of Canon's current dSLR cameras. The camera gets most of the metering information from monitor preflashes emitted from the Speedlite. These preflashes are emitted almost simultaneously with the main flash so it looks as if the flash has only fired once. The camera also uses data from the lens, such as distance information and f-stop values.

2.2 430EX LCD menu set to E-TTL

E-TTL

This is an older form of Canon's flash metering system. It functions very much like E-TTL II. This metering system was used on Canon camera bodies from 1995 up to 2004. Its use stopped with introduction of E-TTL II.

 Note E-TTL and E-TTL II appear as just ETTL on the Speedlite LCD because, although the Speedlite functions in both of these modes, a camera body only uses one type of metering system. Whether it is E-TTL or E-TTL II depends on the camera you are using the Speedlite with.

Caution Canon's older film cameras use a flash metering system known as A-TTL. The 430EX and 580EX flashes are not compatible with this technology and will not work with these cameras.

Manual

Setting the 430EX or 580EX Speedlite to full Manual mode requires you to adjust the settings yourself. The best way to figure this out is by using a formula. You need to know the *Guide Number* (GN) of the Speedlite. The Guide Number is a measure of the flash output. The higher the Guide Number, the more output and range the flash has. You need to know the GN in order to figure out which aperture to use to get the correct flash exposure for the distance your subject is. The formula to get the correct aperture is GN ÷ Distance = Aperture.

Multi stroboscopic flash

In this mode, the flash fires repeatedly like a strobe light during a single exposure. You must manually determine the proper flash output using the formula to get the correct aperture (GN ÷ D = F-stop), and then you decide the frequency and the number of times you want the flash to fire. The slower the shutter speed, the more flashes you are able to capture. For this reason I recommend only using this mode in a low-light situation because the ambient light tends to overexpose the image. Use this mode to create a multiple exposure type image.

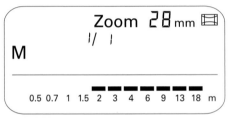

2.3 580EX LCD menu set to Manual full power

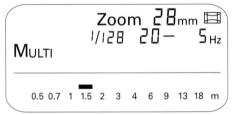

2.5 580EX LCD menu set to Multistroboscopic flash

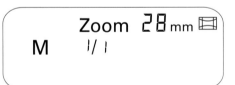

2.4 580EX LCD menu set to Manual full power

Cross-Reference *For more information on how to use this formula in your own photography, see Chapter 3. This formula is covered in depth there.*

To use this mode:

1. **Set the camera to M.**

2. **Press the Mode button on the Speedlite until the Multi menu appears on the LCD.**

3. **Use the 580EX's Sel/Set button in the middle of the dial to highlight the frequency setting.** The frequency is set in *hertz* (Hz). Use the dial change the frequency from 1 to 199 Hz. Hertz is simply a measurement of cycles per second. 1 Hz is one cycle per second.

4. Press the center Set/Sel button again. This sets the frequency level and highlights the number of flashes per frame. Set this to how many times you want the flash to fire per second.

5. Press the center Set/Sel button again. This sets the last option and allows you to set the flash exposure level.

6. Figure out the proper aperture using the GN ÷ D = A formula.

 Cross-Reference *For more on using and understanding the GN ÷ D = A formula, see Chapter 3.*

7. Set your shutter speed. Your shutter speed depends on the firing frequency of the flash per second (measured in Hz) and the number of flashes (also called the *repeat rate*). You can figure out the shutter speed by doing a little math. Your shutter speed is equal to the number of flashes divided by the firing frequency. Sound confusing? It's really not. Say you set the frequency to 5 Hz, and you want the flash to fire 20 times in a single frame, you divide 20 by 5. So you need a 4-second shutter speed.

8. Check the pilot light and then shoot the photo.

Tip *To prevent overexposing moving objects, reduce the aperture by one stop. Otherwise, your moving object is likely to end up overexposed.*

Zoom position

The zoom position focuses the light from the flash in order to match the angle of coverage of your lens. The coverage for wide-angle lenses needs to be wider so the flash head is zoomed back, diffusing the light and allowing it to disperse in a wider area. When a longer lens is used, the light output is focused to allow a further distance to be achieved.

By default the 430EX and 580EX automatically set the zoom to match the lens. I recommend leaving it on the default setting.

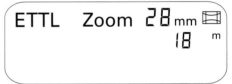

2.6 430EX LCD menu zoom setting 28mm

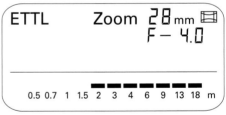

2.7 580EX LCD menu zoom setting 28mm

430EX

To set the zoom manually:

1. Press the Zoom button on the back of the flash. The Zoom setting flashes when it is ready to be changed.

2. **Use the + or – buttons to change the zoom setting.**

3. **When finished, press the Zoom button again to save the setting.** You can also just tap the shutter button to resume shooting.

580EX

To set the zoom manually:

1. **Press the Zoom button on the back of the flash.** The Zoom setting flashes when it is ready to be changed.

2. **Scroll the dial left or right to change the zoom setting.**

3. **When finished, press the Zoom button again to save the setting.** You can also just tap the shutter button to resume shooting.

Adjusting Flash Exposure Compensation

As I discussed previously, you don't always want your Speedlites firing at the same output, which is why it is a good idea to know how to change the flash exposure compensation (FEC) setting. Your camera and Speedlite both take a reading to decide how much output is needed for a perfectly lit exposure. Your camera's idea of a perfect exposure doesn't take into account your artistic vision. This is where you decide how you want your image to look.

Adjusting the output of your Speedlight can be done in a number of different ways. When the Speedlite is mounted on camera, you can adjust the output on the camera body itself. Most Canon dSLRs have a button for setting flash exposure compensation.

You can also adjust the flash output on the Speedlite. Follow these steps to set the flash output on the 430EX:

1. **With the 430EX attached to your camera body in TTL mode, simply press the Set/Sel button for about a half second.** The Flash Exposure Compensation (FEC) icon begins to blink.

2. **Use the + or – buttons to adjust the settings accordingly.**

3. **Press the Set/Sel button to save the setting.**

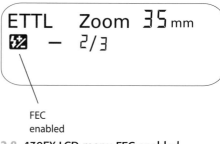

FEC enabled

2.8 430EX LCD menu FEC enabled

To change exposure compensation on the 580EX in TTL mode, follow these steps:

1. **Press the Sel/Set button.** The FEC icon flashes when changes are ready to be made.

Red-Eye Reduction

Red-eye. . . everybody's seen it in a picture at one time or another. The devilish red glare makes your subjects look like they crawled out of the ninth ring of Dante's Inferno. This anomaly is fortunately not caused by demonic possession, but is caused by the reflection of the light from the flash off of the eye's retina (back of the eye). Most cameras that have flash compatibility have a red-eye reduction function, which consists of a preflash or an LED that produces a light bright enough to constrict the pupils, therefore reducing the amount of light reflecting entering the eye and bouncing off of the retina.

Red-eye reduction cannot be set on the 580EX or 430EX. The camera body controls this function. Most, if not all Canon dSLR camera bodies have some sort of red-eye reduction function. Consult your specific camera's owner's manual for instructions on how to set it up.

2. **Scroll the select dial left or right to make the adjustments.**

3. **After your adjustments are made, press the Sel/Set button again to save the setting.**

 Note *When exposure compensation is dialed in, the settings appear on the LCD. When the FEC is returned to normal, the FEC icon does not appear.*

To return the FEC to normal follow the same procedure as in the previous set of steps, and set the Speedlite accordingly.

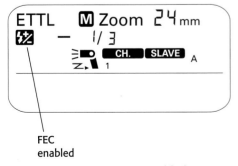

FEC
enabled

2.9 580EX LCD menu FEC enabled

AF Assist Beam

When photographing in a dark environment, it is sometimes hard for your camera's auto-focus sensor to find something to lock on to. When using a 580EX or 430EX in a low-light situation, the flash emits an LED pattern to give your camera sensor something to focus on. For this feature to work, you must be using an AF lens and the camera's focus mode must be set to Single shot or AI Focus.

430EX

Turning the AF-ILL on and off on the 430EX:

1. **Press the C.fn button for two seconds to enter the Custom functions menu.**

2. **Use the + and - buttons to select the C.fn number.** The C.fn number for AF Assist beam OFF is F04. After you select C.fn F04, press the Sel/Set button and the menu blinks.

3. **Use the + or – button to change the setting to either 0 or 1.** 0 is AF Assist beam OFF disabled; this means the beam is ON. 1 means that the AF Assist beam will not come on.

4. **Press the Sel/Set button to save the setting.**

5. **Press the Mode button to return to the main menu.**

580EX

To turn the AF Assist illuminator on and off on the 580EX:

1. **Press the C.fn button for two seconds to enter the Custom functions menu.**

2. **Scroll the dial left or right to select the C.fn number.** The C.fn number for AF Assist beam OFF is F12. After you select C.fn F12, press the Set button in the middle of the dial and the menu blinks.

3. **Scroll the dial left or right to change the setting to either 0 or 1.** 0 is AF Assist beam OFF disabled, this means the beam is ON. 1 means that the AF Assist beam will not come on.

4. **Press the Set button to save the setting.**

5. **Press the Mode button to return to the main menu.**

LCD Panel Illumination

The LCD panels of both the 430EX and 580EX have a light built in to help viewing in low-light situations. To turn on this light, simply press the C.fn button. This LCD light turns off when you press the button a second time or will automatically turn off after approximately 10 seconds.

Auto Off Mode

Both the 580EX and 430EX have an Auto off or standby mode. The Auto off function puts the flash to sleep when not in use. This function helps conserve battery power. When the Speedlite goes in to standby, all you need to do to wake it up is to tap the shutter button or switch the Speedlite off then on again.

The Speedlite defaults have the standby set to automatic. I leave my Speedlites at this setting because it saves battery power and when the flash goes to sleep it only takes a fraction of a second to wake it up again. Of course, you can turn the standby function off by selecting it in the C.fn. This is C.fn 14 on the 580EX and C.fn 02 in the 430EX. Change it using the same method used to change the settings for the AF Assist beam described earlier in this chapter.

Auto Zoom Adjustment for APS-C Sensors

Certain Canon camera bodies, such as the pro-level dSLRs, have a full frame sensor. Which means the digital sensor is exactly the same size as a frame of 35mm film. Canon's consumer-level dSLR's are equipped with an APS-C size sensor, which is a bit smaller than a 35mm frame of film. With this smaller sensor, the actual focal length of the lens doesn't cover the same amount of area as it would on a full-frame sensor or piece of film.

This brings up the lens conversion factor.

Simply stated, you take the actual focal length of the lens and multiply this number by 1.5 to find out the equivalent focal length of the lens in terms of 35mm film. For example, on a full frame camera, a 28mm lens is considered wide angle and is actually a 28mm lens. However, when you multiply it by the lens conversion factor of 1.5, you get the same angle of coverage as a 42mm lens when using the same 28mm lens on a camera with an APS-C size sensor.

Canon Speedlites recognize when they are attached to an APS-C size sensor and adjust the flash head zoom automatically to compensate. When the Speedlite is connected to such a camera an icon appears in the upper right hand corner of the Speedlite LCD.

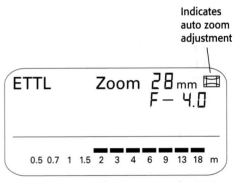

Indicates auto zoom adjustment

2.10 Auto zoom adjustment icon for APS-C size sensors

Creating Great Photos with Your Speedlites

P A R T

II

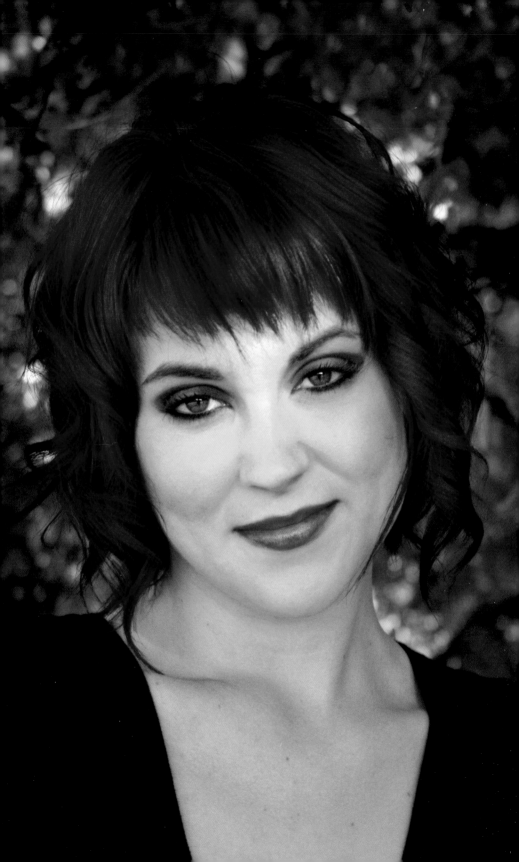

Flash Photography Basics

This chapter goes over some of the basic information you should know when starting out with flash photography. For those of you who aren't new to using external flash or the Speedlite system, much of this may be a review — but you might learn a thing or two about your Speedlites and how to best use them. If you are new to the Speedlite system, then this chapter is a great resource for you and a great reference tool as you experiment and practice with your new Speedlite or Speedlites.

Speedlites versus Studio Strobes

There are many reasons why you'd want to use Speedlites instead of studio strobes. That being said, there are also many reasons to use studio strobes. Each type of light has its own strong points. When deciding what type of lighting to get, you really need to look at what you plan to use it for.

If you know you are traveling with your lighting setup, the portability of the Speedlites comes in handy. If you have a studio and you need a lot of light for big subjects, studio strobes may be the way to go.

This isn't to say you need one or the other. Most professional photographers use both. I own both studio strobes and Speedlites. When I go out to shoot on location, you can bet that I don't drag out those heavy old studio strobes and power packs.

This section discusses the pros and cons of the different lighting systems.

✦ **Portability.** Let's face it, you can pack three or four Speedlites in one bag, which only weighs a few pounds. You still need stands and umbrellas for many types of shooting, but the Speedlites themselves are small and very portable.

✦ **Power.** Speedlites run on AA batteries. You don't have to rely on household current and long extension cords to power these flashes. You can power studio strobes with accessory batteries, but the accessory battery weighs more than the strobes themselves in some cases. That's one more piece of equipment, per strobe, that you have to worry about.

Tip *When first setting up for a studio session, I always put a set of freshly charged rechargeable batteries in each Speedlite I use. I find that one set of batteries can last me for hundreds of photos, often lasting me the entire job. Buying at least one set of extra batteries for each Speedlite you own is a good idea.*

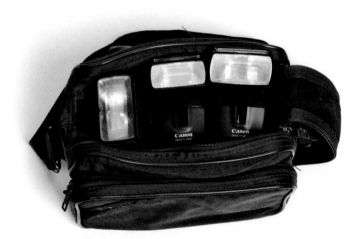

3.1 I use an old camera bag to carry all my Speedlites and accessories.

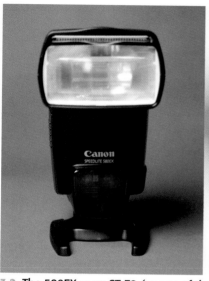
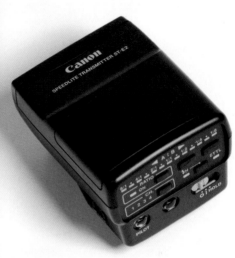

3.2 The 580EX or an ST-E2 (or one of the macro lites) is all you need to control lighting output from multiple Speedlites.

✦ **Ease of use.** After you arrange and configure your Speedlites, you're ready to shoot, controlling flash output centrally. With studio strobes, you have to make all of your adjustments at either the flash head (if using mono-lights) or at the power pack.

✦ **TTL.** With studio strobes, you don't have the advantage of through-the-lens metering. When using the Canon version of TTL metering, E-TTL (ETTL), the camera automatically adjusts the exposure according to the desired flash output and adjusts distance to the subject as calculated from the lens distance setting. This automatic adjustment is a huge advantage of using

Speedlites — you can just basically set up your Speedlites for E-TTL, set the groups and channels, and start shooting. Your Canon camera does the rest. With studio flashes, you have to set up the output for each flash manually.

 Cross-Reference *For information on setting groups and channels, see Chapter 4.*

I'm not one to advocate that using Canon Speedlites is the only way to go for studio lighting, but it's a great start if you're either on a budget or need the advantage of portability. Studio strobes do in fact offer a few advantages over using Speedlites in some studio lighting situations. Here are a few:

✦ **Power.** Studio strobes often offer the photographer more flash power and more light with which to work. In other words, you can illuminate your subjects from greater ranges (Speedlites are limited to less than 100 feet). Many studio strobe models easily provide more light output, which is an advantage if your studio work consists of illuminating large objects (such as automobiles), or even large group portraits. Additionally, you won't have to change batteries as you do when using Speedlites.

✦ **Recycling time.** Recycling time is the amount of time it takes the flash to be ready for another photo. Speedlites typically take .1 to 6 seconds between shots, where studio strobes can fire multiple bursts in that same timeframe.

✦ **Availability of accessories.** Studio strobes offer a much wider range of light directional accessories. Barn doors, snoots, soft-boxes, umbrellas, gels, and diffusers are standard studio strobe accessories. Although most of these accessories can be obtained for Speedlites, they are not widely available, and you may have to special order them. Photographers often rely on mixing and matching these accessories to gain more lighting effects for their work.

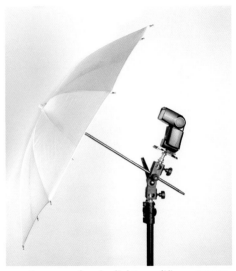

3.3 An example of a light modifier – 480EX with an umbrella attached for diffusion.

✦ **Modeling lights.** Studio strobes have the ability to illuminate the subject before the flash is fired using a modeling light. A modeling light is a second light element in the strobe head that when turned on, simulates the light output of the flash, allowing the photographer to preadjust the lighting to his/her taste. Although the 580EX and 430EX have a modeling light feature, the modeling light isn't continuous so as to allow you to preview the effect at all times.

Note *The modeling light from a Speedlite fires a quick 2.5 second series of flashes. It doesn't provide constant lighting so you can see what you are doing. It also depletes your battery power quickly.*

Even though studio lighting in a more traditional sense does have some advantages over using Speedlites, the ease of use and capability of Speedlites is very appealing to many photographers who normally wouldn't bother with studio strobes. For small studios or when in need of portability, using multiple Speedlites is still a very attractive alternative to traditional studio strobes.

Basics of Lighting

When working with Speedlites, the first attribute you think of is strictly studio and portrait photography. The truth is, using Speedlites can span other types of photographic conditions and can be used to enhance other types of lighting in those situations. Think of the subjects you would normally shoot in a studio: people, pets, still life, and products. In those situations, you can use a mixture of natural light (possibly from a window or skylight) and flash. When using the outdoors as your studio, you can shoot many different types of portraits, still life, and product photos, but you have different lighting options from which to choose. Regardless of whether you are shooting indoors at your home, in a formal studio, or outdoors, using Speedlites have their place in each location and situation.

 You can find additional information on using Speedlites for the specific scenarios within the various categories of photography in Chapter 6.

Having the capability of using multiple Canon Speedlites wirelessly as your main lighting system is great. It's even more beneficial when you understand how using Speedlites can enhance your photography in almost any environment. The last thing you want to do is have all the great equipment available to you without understanding how to apply the gear to your photography. First, consider the different types of studio or outdoor lighting options you can create.

Studio lighting

Whether you're setting up a dedicated space for an elaborate studio for your indoor photography or you're using a temporary setup in your living room, studio lighting concepts are the same. If you're just starting out experimenting with studio lighting, your living room, basement, or garage will do just fine. The most important factor to remember with studio lighting is that you control the light with which you illuminate your subjects; you don't let the light control you.

Placement

When taking photos in a studio, first you need to plan how you want to light your subject. This is where your creativity comes into play. Envision how you want your image to appear and then arrange your lighting accordingly. When planning your photographs, take these concepts into account:

✦ **Visual Impact.** Professional photographers take a lot of portraits and still life images in their everyday work, but the best images contain a combination of a strong subject matter and creative lighting. When setting up your studio photos, you should take color, tone, and lighting all in consideration to create the best image possible. I applied all of these principles as I set up for the shot shown in Figure 3.4. With a little planning, you can maximize the visual impact of your subject or subjects too.

✦ **Direction.** When setting up the lighting of a subject, the direction of the lighting is your key to success. There isn't any rule for the proper direction of the light from your Speedlites. That decision is up to you and how you want the subject to appear in the final image. When shooting portraits or a still life, plan the direction of your main light. You can keep your main light straight on the subject, move it to the left or right, or even place it behind the subject.

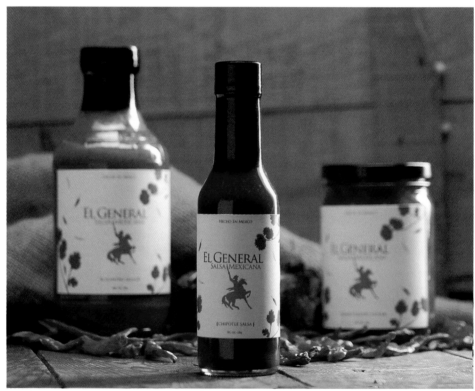

3.4 Plan your studio setup for visual impact, taking color, tone, and lighting into consideration.

✦ **Amount.** You may or may not have heard the terms *high key* or *low key* lighting Simply put, high key lighting is bright and evenly lit, usually having a bright background and a low light ratio of approximately 2:1, as illustrated by Figure 3.5. Conversely, low-key lighting is dramatic lighting, often featuring dark, shadowy areas and ratios of at least 3:1 or higher, which is demonstrated in Figure 3.6. By comparing the images in Figures 3.5 and 3.6 you can see how using high key or low key lighting can completely change the feel of an image.

Tip

You don't have to have three or four Speedlites to set up a studio. Many photographers, even professionals, capture great portraits using one flash, either on or off the camera. If you're using just one Speedlite, consider investing in the Canon Off-Camera Shoe Cord 2. Moving the Speedlite off-camera results in better control over lighting angle, and connecting the Speedlite with this accessory still gives you all the flash-to-camera communication capabilities.

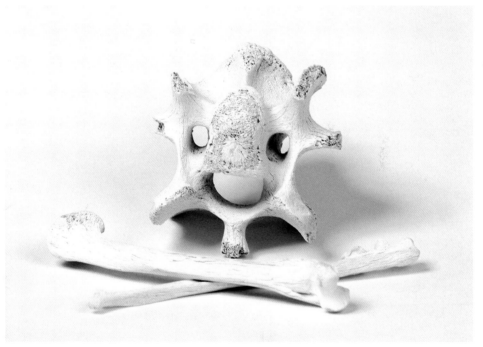

3.5 An example of a high-key image with a high light ratio

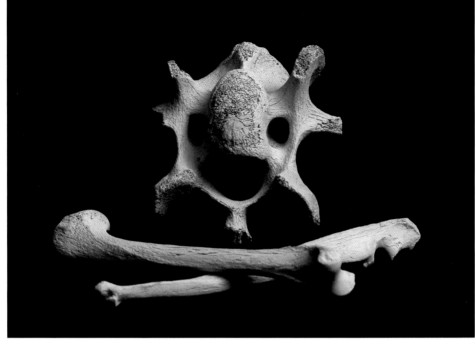

3.6 An example of a low-key image, which uses a low light ratio

Basic portrait lighting types

Two basic types of studio lighting for portraits are *broad* and *short* lighting. If you're a frequent reader of lighting and photography books, you have likely also heard the terms *wide* or *short* lighting. Either way, the two pairs of terms mean the same thing.

Broad or wide lighting refers to a key (main) light illuminating the side of a subject as he or she is turned toward the camera (see figure 3.7). Short lighting, used more frequently, is a key light used to illuminate the side of the subject turned away from the camera (figure 3.8), thus emphasizing facial contours. When using multiple lights, using a fill flash (at a lower power) in conjunction with a key light is common practice.

You may not always be taking portraits in your studio, but that doesn't mean that broad and short lighting techniques do not apply. When shooting portraits outdoors, using the sun as your main light and the Speedlite as a fill, the same rules apply. When the sun is lighting the side of the model facing you, you have broad lighting. When the sun is lighting the side of the model away from you, you have short lighting.

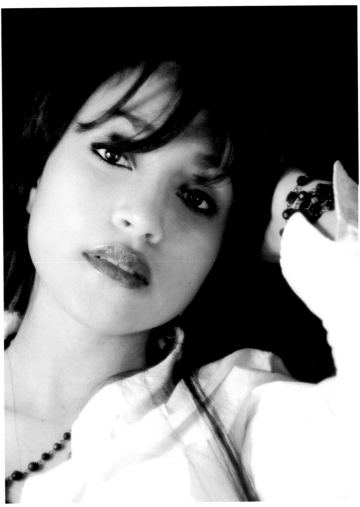

3.7 Broad lighting illuminates the side of the subject that is turned toward the camera.

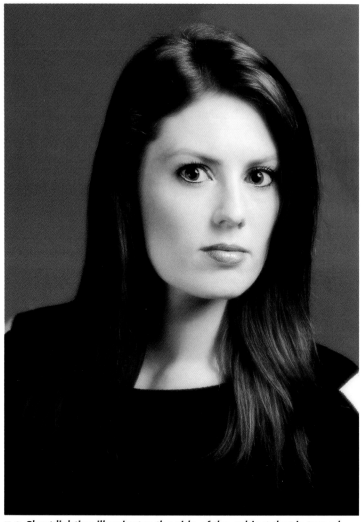

3.8 Short lighting illuminates the side of the subject that is turned away from the camera.

Lighting Ratios

Lighting ratios are the difference in light intensity between the shadow and highlight sides of your subject. Lighting ratios are expressed as any other ratio is, for example, 2:1, which translates as one side being twice as bright as the other. You use ratios when you want to plan how much contrast you want in a portrait or still life. Lighting ratios determine the amount of shadow detail in your images. You can get very accurate measurements for lighting ratios using Speedlites in E-TTL mode. Adjusting ratios is achieved by making adjustments on the master unit for each flash. Here, the figure shows a portrait taken with a 3:1 lighting ratio.

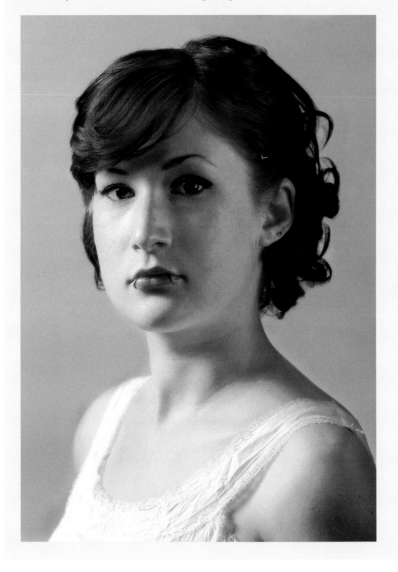

Other types of lighting include:

✦ **Diffused lighting.** Light emitted from a Speedlite can be considered harsh, especially for portraits where the flash is used in close proximity to the subject. *Harsh light* is strong, with a lot of contrast, and when used for portraits, brings out the

worst in skin tones. Harsh light can be too accurate! When taking portraits, bouncing your Speedlite through or from a transparent umbrella or using a diffusion dome over your flash head can help soften the lighting in a portrait, as shown in figures 3.9 and 3.10.

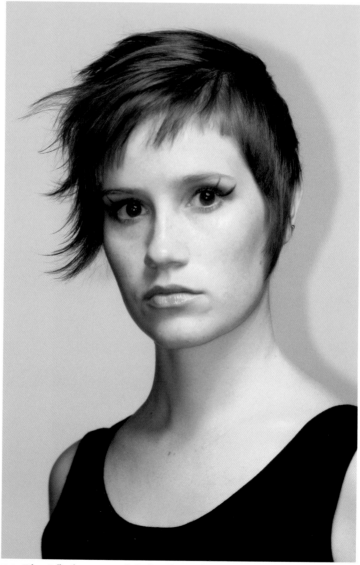

3.9 Direct flash can result in harsh results, especially for portraits. Note the shadow behind the model.

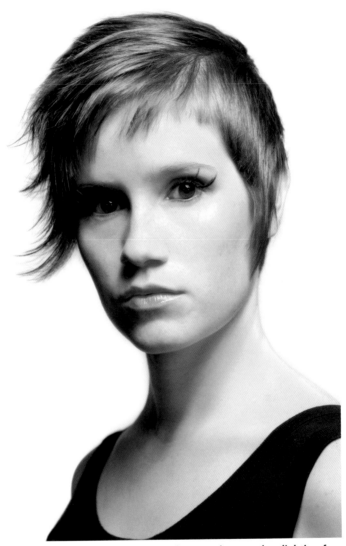

3.10 Diffused flash can result in a softer, much smoother lighting for portraits.

✦ **Frontal lighting.** This type of lighting is a low-key technique to achieve dramatic portraits. The lighting is very soft in nature, where the main light often comes from a single Speedlite attached to the camera.

✦ **Mixing ambient or natural lighting.** You are often faced with mixing the available light in a scene, whether from existing indoor lighting (ambient) or natural lighting (from a window). You may even want to preserve the tone of the existing light, and only use a flash to match the metered reading of the room for enhanced lighting.

✦ **Bounced lighting.** For excellent snapshots on-the-go, point your flash head at a 45-degree angle toward the ceiling. You get a result of an evenly lit subject with a soft, subdued lighting. Bounce flash is often used for photojournalistic images taken during weddings and worked great for snapshots of friends and family. I explain more about bounced lighting later in this chapter.

Using Speedlites outdoors

One of the most important tools you can have for taking outdoor portraits is a Speedlite. The best light to use is what nature provides, but when taking photos of people or pets outdoors, I almost always use a Speedlite as a *fill flash*. Fill flash is using the flash, not as your main source of lighting, but as a secondary light source to fill in the shadows, resulting in an image with less contrast between the shadows and the highlights.

Light diffusers or reflectors are important tools to use for outdoor portraits, or macro shots, but using a Speedlite outdoors for those shooting situations is just as important, if not more important. Advantages of using Speedlites when taking shots outdoors include:

✦ **Creating a fill light.** Using a Speedlite when taking portraits outdoors enables you to create a properly lighted portrait where the subject is lighted and exposed correctly, giving a more professional - looking effect as seen by comparing the images in figure 3.11 and figure 3.12. Using a fill light can be the difference between having your image appear as a snapshot instead of a professional-looking portrait.

✦ **Reducing contrast.** A Speedlite can improve an outdoor portrait in high-contrast situations. Using a Speedlite can help reduce the difference between the shadows and the highlights.

✦ **Providing light in the dark.** Don't limit yourself to outdoor shooting only in the daytime. When using Speedlites, you can take photos outdoors even at night, as shown in the photo in figure 3.11.

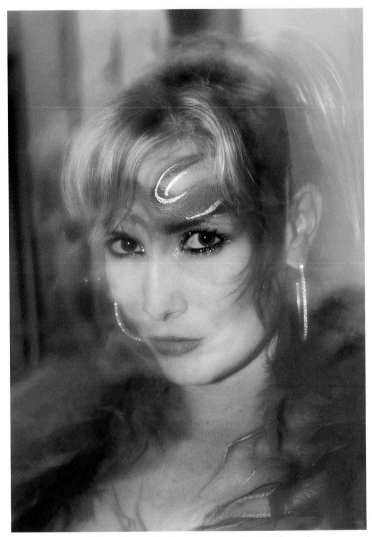

3.11 You can achieve dramatic images even at night by using a Speedlite.

Color Temperature and White Balance

Light, whether it be sunlight, moonlight, fluorescent light, or light from a Speedlite, is measured using the Kelvin scale. This measurement is also known as *color temperature*. One of the advantages of using a digital camera is the ability to measure the color temperature of light through the lens. If your Canon digital camera is set to an automatic light balance, it automatically adjusts the white balance for the shot you are taking. The result of using a correct white balance setting with your digital camera is correct color in your photographs.

What is Kelvin?

Kelvin is a temperature scale, normally used in the fields of physics and astronomy, where absolute zero (0 K) denotes the absence of all heat energy.

Kelvin and color temperature is a tricky concept as it is opposite of what you generally think of as "warm" and "cool" colors. On the Kelvin scale, red is the lowest temperature; increasing through orange, yellow, white, and shades of blue are the highest temperatures. Humans tend to perceive reds, oranges, and yellows as warmer and white and bluish colors to be cold. However, physically speaking the opposite is true as defined by the Kelvin scale. For example, if you think of the hottest part of a flame, it is blue, whereas the cooler parts of the flame are red.

To make this even more confusing, when you set the white balance on your camera using the Kelvin scale, the higher the temperature you select, the redder the image is. What you need to remember is that when you are setting the white balance on your camera, what the camera is actually doing is adding the opposite color of the light that matches the color of the temperature in Kelvin scale, thus making the image neutral.

Preset white balance

Most digital cameras, especially digital SLRs, let you choose the white balance setting manually and even set custom white balance settings. However, generally speaking, automatic white balance settings work well in most situations. The next series of images shows the difference in white balance settings from a photo shot with multiple Speedlites. Each photo represents a different white balance setting, with color temperatures ranging from 2800K to 7500K. The lower the color temperature, the more blue appears in the image. The higher the color temperature, the more red and yellow appear in the image.

Tip *Don't always rely on the automatic white balance settings, especially in mixed light or other difficult lighting situations.*

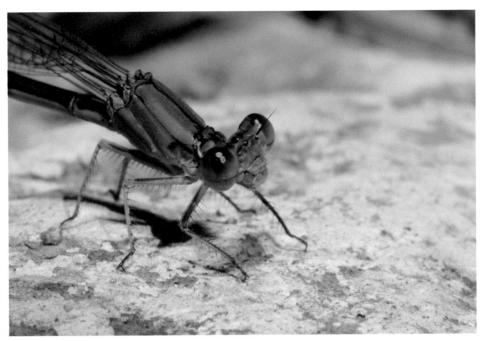

3.12 Tungsten, 2800K

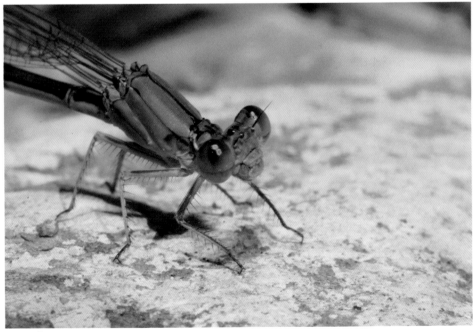

3.13 Fluorescent, 3800K

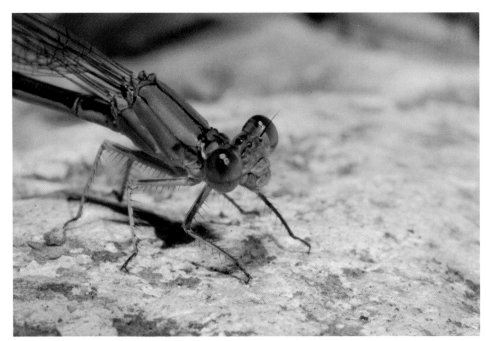

3.14 Auto, 4300K

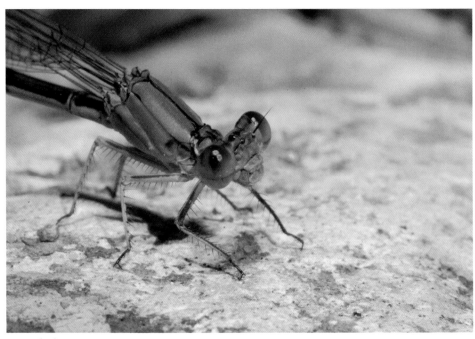

3.15 Flash, 5500K

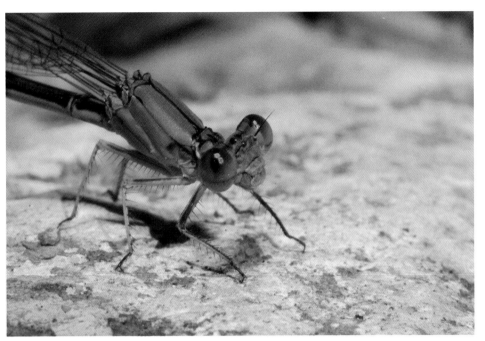

3.16 Daylight, 5500K

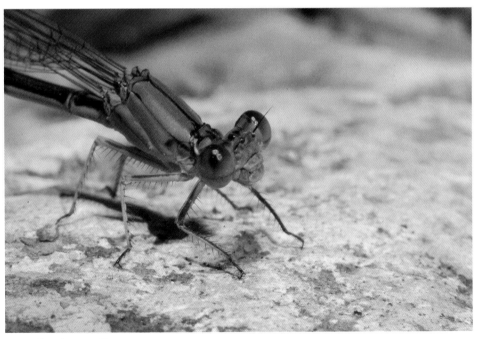

3.17 Cloudy, 6500K

Consider these facts regarding white balance and using Speedlites:

✦ **Speedlites are set to 5500K.**
Speedlites produce light with a color temperature of 5500K, which is also the same color temperature as the daylight white balance setting on Canon dSLRs. When shooting subjects with Speedlites, set the white balance setting on your digital camera to the Flash setting.

✦ **Cooler color temperatures appear blue.** If your digital camera is set to a white balance setting that represents lower color temperatures (below 5000K), your images appear more blue, or cooler.

✦ **Warmer color temperatures appear yellow.** Setting your digital camera to a white balance setting that represents higher color temperatures (above 5000K) makes your images appear more yellow. These images are considered to appear warmer.

✦ **Automatic white balance settings can be very accurate.**
Today's digital cameras perform a very accurate job of measuring a subject's white balance. Setting your digital camera to an automatic white balance setting often results in a correctly color temperature balanced image. When using Auto white balance and a Speedlite with a E-TTL II-compatible digital camera, the Speedlite sends color temperature information to the camera, usually resulting in a more accurate white balance than when set to flash white balance.

Tip
By keeping your digital camera set to the automatic setting, you reduce the amount of images taken with incorrect color temperatures. Most of your images, in many lighting situations (with or without the use of Speedlites) are very accurate. You may discover that your camera's ability to evaluate the correct white balance is more accurate than setting white balance settings manually

✦ **Shoot in RAW format for ultimate control of white balance.**
All Canon digital SLR models offer you the ability to shoot your images in RAW mode. When shooting your images in RAW format (instead of JPEG or TIFF), you have the ability to adjust the white balance of your images after you transfer the files to your computer. By using the RAW conversion software that was included with your digital camera or using Adobe Camera Raw (included with Photoshop CS, CS2, and Photoshop Elements), you can actually adjust the white balance of an image after you take the shot.

Using Bounce Flash

When shooting photos with a Speedlite attached to your camera, you can achieve dramatically different lighting effects by bouncing the light from your flash off the ceiling (or reflector) onto your subject. Bounce flash provides a softer and more evenly lit image.

Bounced flash is a technique used indoors in most situations and can be accomplished a couple of different ways. Most commonly, your flash head needs to be positioned so the light is focused on the ceiling or wall, thus bouncing the light on your subject. Another technique that enables you to bounce flash is with the use of flash umbrellas, a common studio accessory.

When to use bounce flash

You have many situations where a bounced flash is more desirable, especially when taking portraits or snapshots. These situations include:

✦ **Camera is close to the subject.** If you're positioned close to your subject when taking photos, having your Speedlite pointed directly at the subject can result in a washed-out or overlit result. Bouncing the direction of the flash off the ceiling (or even a wall) can help soften the light.

✦ **Even illumination is desired.** If you're taking a photo of a scene where you want more even lighting throughout the frame, bounce flash helps you more evenly illuminate the entire area. Examples are when taking photos where you want both the foreground and background evenly lit. Using a bounced flash results in more balanced lighting in both the foreground and background.

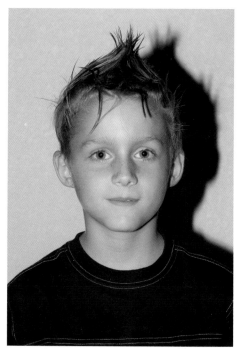

3.18 Close-up portrait using the flash in normal position

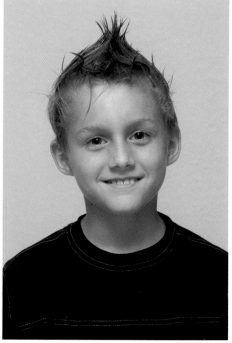

3.19 Close-up portrait using the flash in bounced position

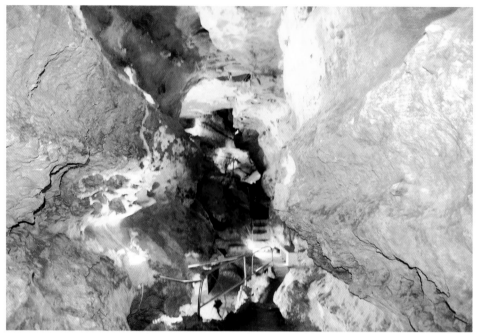

3.20 Interior, Wonder World Cavern, TX, shot with direct flash

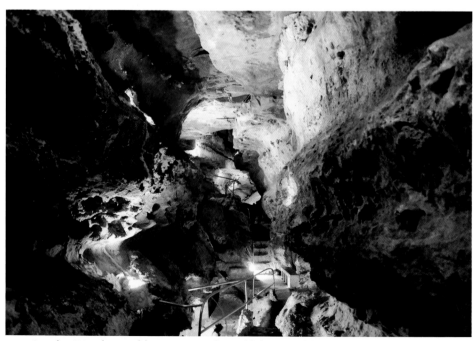

3.21 Interior, Wonder World Cavern, TX, shot with bounced flash

✦ **Shooting portraits.** Directly lit portrait subjects can result in harsh skin tones. Speedlites do a great job in illuminating your subjects, but when it comes to portraits, too good of a job sometimes isn't wanted. A well-exposed portrait using a Speedlite can result in harsh skin tones. To achieve that softened portrait look, bounce your Speedlite off of the ceiling or an umbrella.

Camera and Speedlite settings

When you have the 580EX or 430EX mounted on your camera, you can easily tilt the flash head to bounce the light off the ceiling or even the walls. When bouncing light off the ceiling, position the flash head to a 50- to 60-degree angle. For best results, bounce the flash off surfaces that are 3 to 7 feet from the flash.

When using bounce flash, you need to position your Speedlite flash head, make camera settings, and make adjustments to your Speedlite.

1. **Set your camera's exposure mode to the desired setting.** Whether you prefer using Aperture, Program, Automatic, or Shutter-priority mode, make sure you have your desired exposure mode set in your camera.

2. **Set the white balance.** Set your digital camera's white balance setting to Flash or Auto. Setting your digital camera to a Flash white balance setting fixes the camera at the same color temperature as the light emitted by the Speedlite.

3. **Set the flash mode.** Make sure that the flash mode set on your Speedlite is set to E-TTL. You can toggle to the desired flash mode by pressing the Mode button on your 580EX or 430EX Speedlite.

4. **Position the flash head.** Tilt or rotate the Speedlite's head by pressing the lock release button and positioning the flash head to the desired position. The 580EX Speedlite can tilt up 90° (straight up) and rotate horizontally 180° to the left and right. The 580EX can also be tilted down to -7°. The 430EX can tilt up 90° and rotate horizontally 180° to the left and 90° to the right.

5. **Take a test shot.** Take a photo and review the results on your digital camera's LCD (if you are using a digital camera). If the image appears under- or overexposed, you can adjust the output of the flash by adjusting the flash compensation or by adjusting the aperture setting on your camera. When using bounce flash, you lose two to three stops of light (bouncing light results in less light illuminating the subject as opposed to using normal flash, thus losing two–three stops, measured by aperture settings

To compensate for light loss, you can increase your camera's exposure compensation to increase the amount of light your flash emits to make up for the loss in exposure. Alternatively, you can change your camera's exposure mode to manual and then adjust the aperture setting to stop down your aperture a few stops until you get the desired results.

Explaining Flash Exposure and Specifications

Flash exposure can seem mystifying when you first attempt to use a flash. You need to know a lot of settings and use different formulas to get the right exposure. After you know what the numbers mean and where to plug them, it becomes quite easy.

I start out by explaining the different aspects that involve obtaining the right flash exposure. Of course, if you are using your Speedlite in the E-TTL mode, all of these calculations are done for you, but it's always good to know how to achieve the same results manually. When you know this information, you can use any flash and get excellent results.

In the following sections I explain how to use the guide number, the distance from the Speedlite to the subject, and the aperture to determine the proper flash exposure.

Guide number

The guide number (GN) is a numeric value that represents the amount of light emitted by the flash. You find the GN for your specific Speedlite in the owner's manual. The GN changes with the ISO sensitivity, so that the GN at ISO 400 is greater than the GN of the same Speedlite when set to ISO 100. The GN also differs depending on the zoom setting of the Speedlite. Tables 3.1 and 3.2 break down the guide numbers according to the flash output setting and the zoom range selected on the Speedlite.

Table 3.1
430EX Guide Numbers (at ISO 100)

Flash Coverage (meters/feet)

Flash Output	14	24	28	35	50	70	80	105
1/1	11/ 36.1	25/ 82	27/ 88.6	31/ 101.7	34/ 111.5	37/ 121.4	40/ 131.2	43/ 141.1
1/2	7.8/ 25.6	17.7/ 58.1	19.1/ 62.7	21.9/ 71.9	24/ 78.7	26.2/ 86	28.3/ 92.8	30.4/ 99.7
1/4	5.5/ 18	12.5/ 41	13.5/ 44.3	15.5/ 50.9	17/ 55.8	18.5/ 60.7	20/ 65.6	21.5/ 70.5
1/8	3.9/ 12.8	8.8/ 28.9	9.5/ 31.2	11/ 36.1	12/ 39.4	13.1/ 43	14.1/ 46.3	15.2/ 49.9
1/16	2.8/ 9.2	6.3/ 20.7	6.8/ 22.3	7.8/ 25.6	8.5/ 27.9	9.3/ 30.5	10/ 32.8	10.8/ 35.4
1/32	1.9/ 6.2	4.4/ 14.4	4.8/ 15.7	5.5/ 18	6/ 19.7	6.5/ 21.3	7.1/ 23.3	7.6/ 24.9
1/64	1.4/ 4.6	3.1/ 10.2	3.4/ 11.2	3.9/ 12.8	4.3/ 14.1	4.6/ 15.1	5/ 16.4	5.4/ 17.7

Table 3.2
580EX Guide Numbers (at ISO 100)

Flash Output	*Flash Coverage (meters/feet)*							
	14	**24**	**28**	**35**	**50**	**70**	**80**	**105**
1/1	15/ 49.2	28/ 91.9	30/ 98.4	36/ 118.1	42/ 137.8	50/ 164	53/ 173.9	58/ 190.3
1/2	10.6/ 34.8	19.8/ 65	21.2/ 69.6	25.5/ 83.7	29.7/ 97.4	35.4/ 116.1	37.5/ 123	41/ 134.5
1/4	7.5/ 24.6	14/ 45.9	15/ 49.2	18/ 59.1	21/ 68.9	25/ 82	26.5/ 86.9	29/ 95.1
1/8	5.3/ 17.4	9.9/ 32.5	10.6/ 34.8	12.7/ 41.7	14.8/ 48.6	17.7/ 58.1	18.7/ 61.4	20.5/ 67.3
1/16	3.8/ 12.5	7/ 23	7.5/ 24.6	9/ 29.5	10.5/ 34.4	12.5/ 41	13.3/ 43.6	14.5/ 47.6
1/32	2.7/ 8.9	4.9/ 16.1	5.8/ 17.4	6.4/ 21	7.4/ 24.3	8.8/ 29.9	9.4/ 30.8	10.3/ 33.8
1/64	1.9/ 6.2	3.5/ 11.5	3.8/ 12.5	4.5/ 14.8	5.3/ 17.4	6.3/ 20.7	6.6/ 21.7	7.3/ 24
1/128	1.3/ 4.3	2.5/ 8.2	2.7/ 8.9	3.2/ 10.5	3.7/ 12.1	4.4/ 14.4	4.7/ 15.4	5.1/ 16.7

Tip

If you have access to a flash meter, you can determine the GN of your Speedlite at any setting by placing the meter 10 feet away and firing the flash. Next, take the aperture reading from the flash meter and multiply by ten. This is the correct GN for your flash.

Aperture

Another factor that determines the proper flash exposure is the aperture setting. The wider the aperture, the more light falls on the sensor. The aperture or f-stop number is a ratio showing the fractional equivalent of the opening of the lens compared to the focal length. Are you confused? It's actually pretty simple:

The lens opening at f/8 is the same as 1/8 of the distance of the focal length of the lens. So, if you have a 50mm lens, the lens opening at f/8 is 6.25mm. 50 divided by 8 equals 6.25.

All of the math aside, all you really need to know is this: if your Speedlite output is going to remain the same, in order to lessen the exposure, you need to stop down the lens to a smaller aperture or move the Speedlite further away from the subject.

Distance

The third part in the equation is the distance from the light source to the subject. The closer the light is to your subject the more exposure you have. Conversely, the further away the light source is, the less illumination your subject receives. This is due to the *Inverse Square Law*, which states that the quantity or strength of the light (coming from the Speedlite) landing on your subject is inversely proportional to the square of the distance from the subject to the Speedlite.

In simpler terms, this means you divide one by the distance and then square the result. So if you double the distance, you get 1/2 squared, or 1/4 of the total light; if you quadruple the distance, you get 1/4 squared or 1/16 of the total light. This factor is important because if you set your Speedlite to a certain output, you can still accurately determine the exposure by moving the Speedlite closer or further as needed.

GN ÷ Distance = Aperture

Here's where it all comes together! You take the GN of your flash, divide by the distance away of the subject, and you get the aperture at which you need to shoot. Because you can complete an equation a few different ways, you can change this equation based on the information you already have to find out what you want to know specifically.

✦ Aperture × Distance = GN

✦ Aperture ÷ GN = Distance

✦ GN ÷ Distance = Aperture

Sync speed

The sync speed of your camera is the fastest shutter speed you can shoot with and still get the full exposure of the flash. The sync speed is based on the limitations of the shutter mechanism. The sync speed on different camera bodies differs with the type of shutter mechanism used.

When using Canon Speedlites, the camera body does not let you set the shutter speed faster than the rated sync speed. When a non-dedicated flash or an external strobe is used via the PC sync, it is possible to set your camera to a shutter speed higher than the rated sync speed. The result is an incompletely exposed image.

Fill flash

When shooting outdoors on a sunny day using the sun as your main light source, you usually get images that are very high in contrast. The shadows are invariably much darker than they should be. In order to overcome this, a technique called fill flash is used. When your camera is set to Tv or Av, the camera meter exposes for the ambient light and the Speedlite is used as a fill. When using the Manual setting on your Speedlite, you can also use fill flash.

To do fill flash manually:

1. **Position your subject so that the sun is lighting the subject how you like.** When shooting a portrait, try not to have the sun shining directly in the subject's eyes, as this causes him or her to squint.

2. **Use your camera's light meter to determine the correct exposure.** A typical exposure for a sunny day at ISO 100 is f/16 at 1/125 sec.

3. **Determine the proper exposure for your Speedlite,** Use the GN ÷ Distance = Aperture formula.

> **Note** *You can determine the approximate distance to your subject by looking at the lens after it has been focused on the subject. Most lenses have a distance scale on them or you can use a tape measure.*

4. **After you determine the exposure, set the flash exposure at 1/3 to 2/3 of a stop under the proper exposure.** The actual amount of underexposure needed depends on the brightness of the sun and the darkness of the shadows.

5. **Take the picture and preview it on the LCD.** This helps you to decide if you need more or less flash exposure to fill in the shadows. Change the exposure compensation and take another photograph if you aren't satisfied.

> **Note** *Be sure the flash head zoom is set to the proper focal length for the lens in use.*

Wireless Flash Photography with the Speedlite System

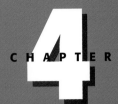
You're probably wondering in what situations might you want to use multiple wireless Speedlites. Well, the answer is you can use them for almost any type of photography and in many different situations. For portraits, you need to be able to move your lights around in order to get the best lighting or specific lighting patterns. You need to be able to adjust your fill light to create a mood. In action photography, if you know where the action is taking place, you can set up your Speedlites at that location and move around to capture different angles without changing the direction or output of your light. When doing still life photography, you can set up two or more Speedlites to fill in the shadows and bring out texture and detail. In architectural photography, you may need to set up a couple of Speedlites to illuminate dark corners so that your overall lighting coverage is even.

As you can see, there are many practical applications for multiple wireless flash units. If you have a need to light it, you can probably think of a way that wireless flash can make it easier for you. After you get the Speedlite off of the camera, you can start to be more creative in shaping the light on your subject. The fact that there are no wires and no need for electrical outlets is an added bonus.

With the Canon Speedlite System, gone are the days of carrying around an expensive light meter, reading the output of each single strobe, and making adjustments on the power pack that the strobe heads are attached. The camera working in conjunction with the master unit does all the metering for you. The camera gets you in the ballpark; all you have to do is fine-tune. The fine-tuning is made easy with the Speedlite system also. All of your adjustments are made from right behind the camera on the 580EX master flash or the ST-E2 transmitter with just one glance at your LCD preview.

The Canon Speedlite System is a very complex tool, but all of the complexities are taken care of within the camera system itself. The Speedlite System takes twenty minutes' worth of metering and adjusting and does it all for you in a matter of milliseconds. You can use all this saved time to come up with more creative images.

This chapter provides an overview of how the Canon Speedlite System uses the camera and master unit to communicate with the remote units, resulting in almost perfect exposures every time.

How the Speedlite System Works Wirelessly with Your Camera

Basically, the Canon Speedlite System is a communication device. When the flash is set to E-TTL, the camera body relays information to the Speedlite you designate as the master unit. The master unit then tells the remotes what to do. The camera's shutter opens and the remotes fire. Sounds fairly simple, doesn't it? And, in all actuality, it is for you, but it's definitely a great feat of electronic engineering.

Broken down into more detail, the whole system is based on pulse modulation. *Pulse modulation* is a fancy term for the Speedlite firing rapid bursts of light in a specific order. Using these pulses, the master unit, be it a 580EX or ST-E2 Speedlite Transmitter, conveys instructions to the remote units.

The first instruction the master sends out to the remotes is to fire a series of monitor preflashes to determine the exposure level. These preflashes are read by the camera's TTL metering sensors, which combine readings from all of the separate groups of Speedlites along with a reading of the ambient light.

The camera tells the master unit what the proper exposure needs to be. The master unit then, via pulse modulation, relays specific information to each group about how much exposure to give the subject. The camera then tells the master when the shutter is opened, and the master unit instructs the remote flashes to fire at the specified output.

All this is done in a split second. Of course when you press the Shutter button, it looks like the flashes fire instantaneously. There's no waiting for the shutter to fire while the Speedlites do their calculations.

Overview of Flash Setup with the Canon Speedlite System

When setting up for a photo shoot, you first need to decide how many Speedlites you want to use. For most small projects, you need at least two Speedlites, one for your main or key light and one for a fill light. But, how many you use depends on what you are doing. For example, when taking portraits you may want to use as many as four Speedlites: one for your key light, one for your fill, one for a background light, and one for a hair light. This can mean using up to five Speedlites, including one to be used as a master unit. This is, of course, an extreme example. You can achieve great results using the ST-E2 as a master and just one Speedlite.

Step 1: Choose a flash mode

Now you need to decide which flash mode you want to use. The two main flash modes available when using the Speedlite System are E-TTL automatic flash and M or manual. I recommend using E-TTL auto flash, as it gets you as close as you need to be without the need for making endless adjustments. The Manual setting is almost the same as using studio strobes. You need to make exposure calculations to decide what to set the output levels.

 Cross-Reference *For more specifics on using the Flash modes, see Chapter 2.*

Step 2: Choose a channel

After you decide which flash mode you want to use, the next step is to decide which channel you want to work on. This decision should be fairly simple. For the most part, it's unlikely you'll be working in close proximity to other photographers, so you can use whatever channel you'd like. In the unlikely event you are working near another photographer using Canon Speedlites wirelessly, just ask them which channel they're using and use a different one. Essentially, it really makes no difference what channel you use as long as there are no other photographers near you using Canon Speedlites wirelessly.

 Note *Be sure all Speedlites are set to the same channel or they won't function properly.*

Step 3: Set up groups or Slave IDs

The next step is setting up groups, also known as Slave IDs. Generally, you want to set your main lights to group A; the fill lights to group B; and any peripheral lights, such as hair and background lights to group C. You want to do it this way so you can adjust the output of the specific lights based on their functions. Your main light is the brightest; probably pretty close to whatever E-TTL reading your camera comes up with. The fill lights need to be a little under what the E-TTL reading is, so by setting them to group B you can adjust the ratios without altering the exposure of your main lights. The background lights may or may not need to be adjusted depending on the darkness of the background, whether you're shooting high key or low key, and so on. You want these lights in group C to enable you make the necessary adjustments without affecting the other two exposures.

Step 4: Adjust the flash ratio levels

Now you're ready to adjust the flash ratio levels. After you get your channels set, your groups decided, and your lights set up, it's time to take some test shots. If you have everything set to the E-TTL flash mode, you should be pretty close to the proper exposure. Just make some minor adjustments to the flash ratios and you're done. All these adjustments can be made right at the camera, so there's no need to visit each light to make minor changes.

In the following sections, you go step-by-step through setting up your flashes for master and remote use, choosing a flash mode, setting channels and groups, and adjusting the output ratios for your specific needs.

Setting Up Masters and Remotes

This part is where you get into the tech stuff: How to set up the Speedlite as a master flash or a wireless remote flash (slave), how to adjust the exposure to suit your needs, setting up groups of lights, and so on. You

are no doubt beginning to see just how versatile and powerful a tool Canon's Speedlite system can be.

You can control an infinite amount of flashes (if you can afford to buy them) all from your camera. You don't even need to have a light meter; the camera meters for you. If you don't like the way the light looks, you can change the flash output without having to walk across the room to a power pack. This is all very convenient.

Masters

The first thing you need to do when setting out to use the Speedlite system wirelessly is set up a commander unit also known as a *master flash*. The master flash is what controls all of the wireless slaves and tells them what to do. The master can be a 580EX or an ST-E2 Speedlite Transmitter. The 430EX can only be used as a slave during wireless operation.

 Note *The MR-14EX and the MT-24EX macro flashes can also be used to control off camera slaves.*

Setting up the 580EX

To use the 580EX as a master flash:

1. **Turn on the Speedlite.** Slide the On/Off switch to the on position.

2. **Set the wireless selector switch to MASTER.** This sets the Speedlite to function as a master unit.

Note *When setting up the Speedlites, you generally set all of the settings in one trip through the Custom Settings Menu. If you need to go back and change any settings, some steps will need to be repeated.*

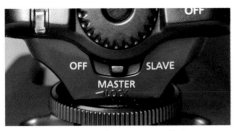

4.1 Be sure to set the 580EX switch to MASTER.

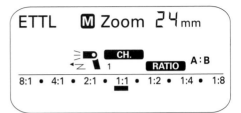

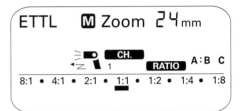

4.2 580EX ratio settings

3. **Press the ZOOM button.** This selects the flash head zoom range so it can be changed. When it is ready to change, it blinks. Set the flash head zoom range to match the focal length of the lens you are using with the Select dial.

> **Note** *When in wireless mode the auto zoom function of the Speedlite is disabled.*

4. **Press the ZOOM button again.** This sets the zoom and highlights the ratio setting for change. Use the selector dial to change the setting. Choose from ratio off, ratio A:B, or ratio A:B C.

> **Note** *When using only one group of Speedlites, set to ratio off. When using two groups, set to ratio A:B. When using three groups, set to ratio A:B C.*

5. **Press the ZOOM button to highlight the channel settings.** Use the selector dial to change the setting from channels 1 through 4.

6. **Press the ZOOM button again to highlight the master flash output setting.** Use the selector dial to turn the flash output on or off. Select the OFF position if you don't want the master flash to add to the exposure.

7. **Press the ZOOM button to finish or if ratio was selected, to set the A:B ratio numbers.** Scroll the dial left or right to set the flash ratio. The flash ratio can be set from 8:1 to 1:1 to 1:8.

To set the output level for Group C when using three groups of Speedlites, set the ratio to A:B C. When everything else is set press the SEL button in the center of the selector dial until ratio C is blinking, and then scroll the dial left or right to adjust the FEC. This can be adjusted in 1/3 stops to +/- 3 stops of light. With no exposure compensation Group C fires at the same output as Group B.

Understanding Flash Ratios in the Canon Speedlite System

When setting the ratios for your wireless Speedlites, you are given quite a few options. The ratios are adjustable in increments of one-half of a stop allowing you thirteen separate settings. This allows you a total of +/- 3 stops of light.

In the center position is the ratio 1:1. This means that the Speedlites in Group A and the Speedlites in Group B both fire at the same output. Adjusting the ratio to 2:1 means that the Speedlites in Group A fire at twice the output as Group B. Conversely adjusting the ratio 1:2 means that Group B fires at twice the power of Group A.

Group C fires at the same output as Group B when used in ratio A:B C. Use FEC to adjust Group C to fit your specific needs.

 Cross-Reference *For instructions on setting up Speedlites as wireless slaves, see Chapter 2.*

 Note *The first number in each ratio always refers to Speedlites in Group A and the second number of the ratio always refers to Speedlites in Group B.*

Setting up the ST-E2

Setting up the ST-E2 is a breeze. All of the necessary changes can be made in a minute. The buttons on the back of the ST-E2 are all labeled clearly with what they do.

1. **Attach the ST-E2 to your camera hot shoe.**

2. **Turn the ST-E2 on using the power switch.**

3. **Select the proper channel using the channel button.** The channel number is lit when selected.

4. **To turn on the ratio feature press the button labeled RATIO.** The Ratio ON button lights up when activated.

5. **Adjust the flash ratio settings using the left and right arrow buttons.** The light under the ratio is lit when selected.

6. **Turn on FP high speed sync by pressing the button with the flash symbol next to an H.**

 Note *To lock the settings on the ST-E2 to prevent them from being changed, slide the power button to the HOLD position.*

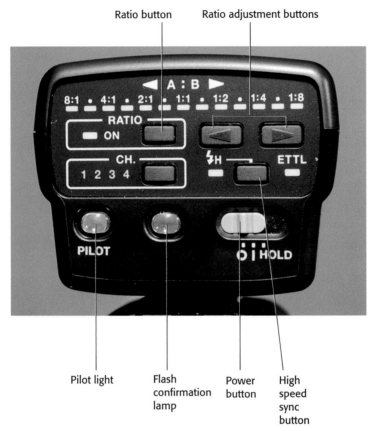

Ratio button   Ratio adjustment buttons

Pilot light   Flash
confirmation   Power   High
lamp   button   speed
sync
button

4.3 Control panel of the ST-E2

Remote flashes

The wireless remote flash is the main advantage of Canon's Speedlite system. It's all about getting the flash off of your camera. By doing this, you are able to control the light in a much better way. You don't have to have full frontal light. You can place a 430EX off to the side in order to accent your models features better or place a 580EX above an object to highlight the texture. The possibilities are endless.

Setting up the 430EX

To set up the 430EX for use as a wireless remote slave flash:

1. **Set the switch on the back of the Speedlite to SLAVE.** This enters the slave settings menu.

2. **Press the ZOOM button to highlight the setting you want to change.** These settings include the flash head zoom range (24mm–105mm), the communication channel (1–4), and the Slave ID (A, B, or C). When the specific setting is ready to be changed, it blinks.

3. **Set the zoom.** Use the + or minus buttons to set the flash head zoom to match the focal length of the lens you're using.

4. **Set the channel.** Use the + or − buttons to set the channel on which the flashes communicate with each other.

 Note *Both the Master and the Slave must be set to the same channel for wireless flash to work.*

5. **Set the Slave ID or group.** You can set up to three different groups of Speedlites, A, B, or C.

Setting up the 580EX

To set up the 580EX for use as a wireless remote flash:

1. **Set the switch on the back of the Speedlite to SLAVE.** This enters the slave settings menu.

2. **Press the ZOOM button to highlight the setting you want to change.** These settings include the flash head zoom range (24mm–105mm), the communication channel (1–4), and the Slave ID (A, B, or C). When the specific setting is ready to be changed, it blinks.

3. **Set the zoom.** Scroll the dial left or right to set the flash head zoom to match the focal length of the lens you're using.

4. **Set the channel.** Scroll the dial left or right to set the channel on which the flashes communicate with each other.

 Note *Both the Master and the Slave must be set to the same channel for wireless flash to work.*

5. **Set the Slave ID or group.** You can set up to three different groups of Speedlites, A, B, or C.

 Note *Slave ID only needs to be set when using two or more groups of flashes.*

Setting Up Wireless Manual Flash

The flash mode is used to decide how the Speedlites are going to be set to the proper exposure level. In the E-TTL mode, the remote flashes fire test shots and the camera meters it through the lens using its exposure sensor and then sets the output for you. In the M mode, you need to decide the proper exposure by using a light meter or the guide number / Distance = Aperture equation. You can input the proper exposure levels into the master unit and the master tells the remotes at what power level to fire.

 Cross-Reference *Chapter 3 explains in detail the guide number/Distance = Aperture equation.*

580EX in Manual mode

To set up for Manual wireless flash on the 580EX in Master mode, follow these steps:

1. **Turn on the Speedlite.** Slide the On/Off switch to the ON position. Be sure the flash mode is set to M. Select this by pressing the MODE button.

2. **Set the wireless selector switch to MASTER.** This sets the Speedlite to function as a master unit.

3. **Press the ZOOM button.** This selects the flash head zoom range so it can be changed. When ready to change, it blinks. Set the flash head zoom to match the focal length of the lens you are using.

4. **Press the ZOOM button again.** This sets the zoom and highlights the ratio setting so it can be changed. Use the selector dial to choose from ratio off, ratio A:B, or ratio A:B C.

> **Note** *When using only one group of Speedlites, set the ratio to ratio off. When using two groups, set the ratio to ratio A:B. When using three groups, set the ratio to ratio A:B C.*

5. **Press the ZOOM button to highlight the channel settings.** Use the selector dial to choose from channels 1 through 4.

6. **Press the ZOOM button again to highlight the master flash output setting.** Use the selector dial to turn the flash output on or off. Select the off position if you don't want the master flash to add to the exposure.

7. **Press the Sel/Set button in the center of the dial to choose the group.** When the group letter is blinking, use the dial to set the desired output level. Press the Select button after you are done to move to next group. Repeat until all groups are set to the output level you have determined.

Setting slaves for manual flash

You can also set your slave units to function entirely manually as you would with studio strobes. Changes must be made on the slave itself; any changes made on the master unit do not affect the output of the slaves.

Essentially, you can get the same results when using the Master in manual mode. I prefer to use the other method because when you use this feature, all of the changes are made on the slave unit, which can be time-consuming. However, it is up to you to determine which method works best for you and your workflow.

When determining the exposure, you need a handheld flash meter or you have to use the GN/D=A equation.

Setting the 430EX as a manual slave

1. **Turn on the Speedlite.**

2. **Switch the Wireless selector to SLAVE.**

3. **Press and hold the Mode button for two seconds.** This sets the flash to manual slave mode. You see a blinking M on the LCD.

4. **Press and hold the Sel/Set button for one second.** The M and the power level blink.

5. **Set the power level output using the + or − buttons.** The power level can be set to 1/1 or full power all the way down to 1/64 power.

6. **Press the Sel/Set button to save the power setting.**

Setting the 580EX as a manual slave

1. **Turn on the Speedlite.**

2. **Switch the Wireless selector to SLAVE.**

3. **Press and hold the Mode button for two seconds.** This sets the flash to manual slave mode. You see a blinking M on the LCD.

4. **Press and hold the Sel/Set button for one second.** The M and the power level blinks.

5. **Set the power level output using the + or − buttons.** The power level can bet set to 1/1 or full power all the way down to 1/128 power.

6. **Press the Sel/Set button to save the power setting.**

Using Wireless Multi Stroboscopic Flash

You can use your 580EX to fire a Slave using the Multi Stroboscopic Flash mode. Although the 430EX does not have the ability to do Multi flash on its own, when used as a slave with the 580EX as a master, this function is available to you.

Note *Multi Stroboscopic Flash is not available when using the ST-E2 as a master.*

Cross-Reference *For more information on wireless Multi Stroboscopic Flash, see Chapter 2.*

Setting Up Channels and Groups or Slave IDs

In this section you look at how to set channels and slave IDs to be used with wireless flash.

Channels

When using a Speedlite in the wireless mode, you can choose on which channel your master unit communicates with the slave. You have four channels from which to choose. This feature is included because sometimes professionals can be shooting where other photographers are using the same equipment. In order to prevent another photographer's Speedlites from setting off your own (and vice-versa), you can set your remote commander to a different channel.

Channel settings are changed in the Speedlite slave settings menu, which was explained earlier in this chapter.

Setting groups

When using more than one Speedlite, you want to set up your Speedlites in separate groups in order to adjust the lighting for each group to different levels. Setting each group to different levels enables you to achieve three-dimensional lighting. When all of the Speedlites are set the same, the lighting is flat and even. For some subjects this is good, but for other subjects you want to vary the light output in order to show texture and contour. For example, when shooting an object such as a circuit board, you want the lighting to be nice and even so you can see all of the details with clarity. On the other hand, when photographing a portrait, you want to show depth and have a varied tonality, so you want your main light, commonly set to Group A to be brighter than your secondary fill light (Group B). To achieve this, you adjust your fill light so that the output is less than the main light. When the Speedlites are set to different groups, you can adjust one without making changes to the other.

> **Note** The Channel and Slave ID setting must be set on each individual Speedlite in order for them to function properly.

430EX

To set up channels and slave IDs using the 430EX:

1. **Turn the Speedlite on using the On/Off switch.**

2. **Set the Wireless selector switch to SLAVE.**

3. **Press the Zoom button until the SLAVE ID is blinking on the LCD.**

4. **Use the + or - to select the slave ID.** Choose from A, B, or C.

5. **Press the ZOOM button again until the Channel setting is blinking.**

6. **Use the + or – buttons to select the channel.** Choose from channels 1, 2, 3, or 4.

7. **Press the Sel/Set button to save the settings.**

580EX

To set channels and Slave IDs using the 580EX:

1. **Turn the Speedlite on using the On/Off switch.**

2. **Set the Wireless selector switch to SLAVE.**

3. **Press the Zoom button until the SLAVE ID is blinking on the LCD.**

4. **Use the (select dial) to select the slave ID.** Choose from A, B, or C.

5. **Press the ZOOM button again until the Channel setting is blinking.**

6. **Use the (select dial) buttons to select the channel.** Chose from channels 1, 2, 3, or 4.

7. **Press the select button in the middle of the select dial to save the settings.**

Setting Flash Exposure Compensation

You use Flash Exposure Compensation (FEC) to fine-tune the settings to achieve the desired brightness of the overall image. The FEC can be adjusted in one-third increment stops, up to +3 and down to -3 stops of light.

 Note *When the FEC is set on the master flash, the exposure compensation affects all the slave Speedlites.*

With the 580EX set to Master

To set flash exposure compensation, follow these steps:

1. **Turn on the Speedlite.**

2. **Be sure the Wireless selector switch is set to MASTER.**

3. **Press the Sel/Set button in the middle of the selector dial.** This brings up the FEC compensation menu. It blinks when ready to change.

 Note *When the FEC is set to 0, the FEC icon does not appear on the LCD unless it selected for change.*

4. **Scroll the selector dial left or right to adjust the output level.**

5. **Press the Sel/Set button in the middle of the selector dial to set the FEC.**

 Note *When setting the FEC on the 580 EX, setting to MASTER adjusts the output on ALL slave flashes.*

Setting FEC on slave flashes

When using the ST-E2 wireless transmitter, the FEC must be set on the slave flash.

580EX

To change exposure compensation on the 580EX in slave mode, follow these steps:

1. **Press the Sel/Set button.** The FEC icon flashes when changes are ready to be made.

2. **Scroll the select dial or right to make the adjustments.**

3. **After your adjustments are made, press the Sel/Set button again to set.**

430EX

To change exposure compensation on the 430EX in slave mode, follow these steps:

1. **Press the Set/Sel button for about a half second.** The Flash Exposure Compensation (FEC) icon begins to blink.

2. **Use the + or – buttons to adjust the settings accordingly.**

3. **Press the Set/Sel button to save the setting.**

Setting Up a Wireless Studio

A portable studio is a handy thing to have. It enables you to go on location and photograph your subjects in their own environment. This way you can take your studio to your client. A portable studio should be exactly that — portable. You should be able to fit everything you need into a minimum amount of space and be able to transport it quickly and with little effort.

The great thing about the Canon Speedlite system is that it enables you to make your portable studio even more portable and easier to set up. You no longer need bulky studio lights in order to create professional-looking images. The Canon 430EX and 580EX are small and affordable, and best of all they can be used wirelessly off-camera.

Introduction to the Portable Studio

A portable studio should include, but should not be limited to at least one Speedlite, a reflector of some sort to fill in the harsh shadows created by strobes, an umbrella or softbox to soften the light for a more pleasing effect, and one or more light stands.

Note *The 430EX functions as a remote flash only when using the Speedlite system. It cannot be used as a commander for other flash units.*

Ideally, your portable studio has at least two or more Speedlites, depending on the types of subjects you shoot. Also handy, but not absolutely necessary for all subjects, are backgrounds and background stands.

Tip *Although I recommend using a professional reflector disk, you can use lots of different items as a reflector. White foam board (available at any art supply store) works particularly well. In a pinch almost anything white or silver works—a lid from a Styrofoam cooler or even a white t-shirt.*

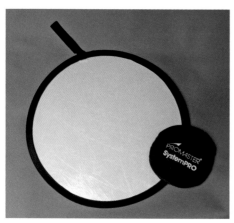

5.1 These reflector disks fold up to a very convenient size.

Choosing Umbrellas

Photographic umbrellas are basically the same as an umbrella you would use to keep the raindrops from falling on your head, but photographic umbrellas are coated with a material to maximize reflectivity. Photographic umbrellas are used to diffuse and soften the light that is emitted from the light source, be it continuous or strobe lighting.

If you are already familiar with the various pieces of studio photography equipment, you likely already know that umbrellas do almost all of the same thing that a softbox does. What you may not know is that umbrellas are more affordable and are easier to use than softboxes, as an accessory for your Canon Speedlite. (This isn't to say, though, that softboxes aren't useful—they are.)

The three types of umbrellas to choose from are

✦ **Standard.** The most common type of umbrella has a black outside with the inside coated with a reflective material that is usually silver or gold in color. These are designed so that you point the Speedlite into the umbrella and bounce the light onto the subject, resulting in a non-directional soft light source.

✦ **Shoot-through.** Some umbrellas are manufactured out of a one-piece translucent silvery nylon that enables you to shoot through the umbrella, like a softbox. You can also use this type of umbrella to bounce the light, as mentioned previously.

✦ **Convertible.** The third type of umbrella is a convertible umbrella. This umbrella has a silver or gold lining on the inside and a removable black cover on the outside. You can use these umbrellas to bounce light or as a shoot-through when the outside covering is removed.

Photographic umbrellas come in various sizes usually ranging from 27 inches all the way up to 12½ feet. The size you use is dependent on the size of the subject and the degree of coverage you would like to get. For standard headshots, portraits, and small to medium products, umbrellas ranging from 27 inches to about 40 inches supply plenty of coverage. For full-length portraits and larger products, a 60- to 72-inch umbrella is generally recommended. If you're photographing groups of people or especially large products, you will need to go beyond the 72-inch umbrella.

The larger the umbrella, the softer the light falling on the subject from the Speedlite is. It is also true that the larger the umbrella, the less light that falls on your subject. Generally the small-to-medium umbrellas lose about a stop and half to two stops of light. Larger umbrellas generally lose two or more stops of light because the light is being spread out over a larger area.

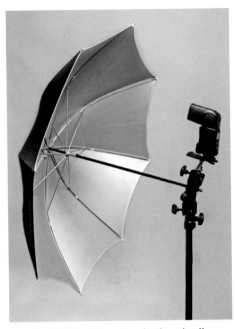

5.2 An 430EX with a standard umbrella

Smaller umbrellas tend to have a much more directional light than do larger umbrellas. With all umbrellas, the closer you have the umbrella to the subject the more diffuse the light is.

For setting up a wireless/portable studio, I'm convinced that the umbrella is the way to go. They fold up nice and small, are simple to use, are relatively inexpensive, and attach to the light stand with an inexpensive bracket which is available at any photography store for less than $15. This bracket also includes a shoe mount for attaching your Speedlite.

Choosing the right umbrella is a matter of personal preference. Some criteria to keep in mind when choosing your umbrella include the type, size, and portability. You also want to consider how it works with your Speedlite. For example, regular and convertible umbrellas return more light to the subject when bounced, which can be advantageous because a Speedlite has less power than a studio strobe. And, the less energy the Speedlite has to output, the more battery power you save. On the other hand, shoot-through umbrellas lose more light through the back when bouncing, but are generally more affordable than convertible umbrellas.

Using a Softbox

Softboxes, as with umbrellas, are used to diffuse and soften the light of a strobe to create a more pleasing light source. Softboxes range in size from small 6-inch boxes that you mount directly onto the flash head to large boxes that usually mount directly to a studio strobe. Softboxes come in a variety of shapes, too — anywhere from a small, square shaped softbox to very large, octagonal softbox designed to simulate umbrellas.

Flash-mount softboxes

The small flash-mounted softboxes are very economical and easy to use. You just attach it directly to the flash head and use it with your flash mounted on the camera or on a flash bracket. This type of softbox is good to use while photographing an event, informal portraits, wedding candids, or just plain old snapshots of your friends and family. You generally lose about one stop of light with these and should adjust your flash exposure compensation accordingly. For shooting small still life subjects or simple portraits, this may be all you need to get started with your wireless/portable studio.

Stand-mounted softboxes

When photographing in a studio type of setting, you really need a larger softbox that is mounted, along with your Speedlite, onto a suitable light stand. For a larger softbox, you need a sturdier stand to prevent the lighting setup from tipping over. Bogen/Manfrotto, manufacturers of high-quality stands and tripods, have a basic six foot stand that works well for this application.

The reason that you may want to invest in a softbox rather than an umbrella for your portable studio is that softboxes provide a more consistent and controllable light than umbrellas do. Softboxes are closed around the light source thereby eliminating unwanted light from being bounced back on to your subject. The diffusion material gives less of a chance of creating hotspots on your subject. A *hotspot* is an overly bright spot on your subject usually caused by bright or uneven lighting.

Softboxes are generally made for use with larger studio strobes. They attach to these strobes with a device called a *speedring*. Speedrings are specific to the type of lights to which they are meant to attach. Luckily for photographers, some companies, such as Chimera, manufacture a type of speedring that mounts directly to the light stand and allows you to attach one or more

Speedlites to the light stand as well. You mount the speedring to the stand, attach the softbox to the speedring, attach the Speedlite with the flash head pointed into the softbox, and you're ready to go.

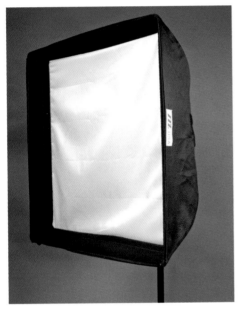

5.3 Stand-mounted softbox

Stand-mounted softboxes come in a multitude of shapes and sizes ranging from squares to rectangles to ovals to octagons. Most photographers use standard square or rectangular softboxes. However, some photographers prefer to use oval or octagonal ones for the way that they mimic umbrellas and give a more pleasing round shape to the catchlights in the eyes. This is mostly a matter or personal preference. I, for one, usually use a medium-sized rectangular softbox.

As with umbrellas, the size of the softbox you need to use is dependent on the subject you are photographing. Softboxes can be taken apart and folded up pretty conveniently—most of them come with storage bag that you can use to transport them.

Softbox alternatives

If you are working on a budget, or just aren't sure you are ready to invest in a softbox, a more economical approach is to use a diffusion panel. A *diffusion panel* is basically a frame made out of PVC pipe with a reflective nylon stretched over it. It functions much in the same way as a softbox, but you have more control over the quality of the light. Because the PVC frame can be disassembled easily and packed away into a small bag for storage or for transport to and from a location, it makes it great for the portable studio.

Diffusion panels are usually about six feet tall and have a base which allows it to stand up without the need of a light stand. The diffusion panel is placed in front of the subject. Your Speedlite is then mounted on a light stand using the adaptor/stand that is supplied with it. You can move the Speedlite closer to the diffusion panel for more directional light or further away for a softer and more even light. For a full-length portrait, you should place two Speedlites behind the panel, one near the top and one closer to the bottom.

A diffusion panel can also be used as a reflector when used in conjunction with another light source. Diffusion panels can be purchased at most major camera stores at a fraction of the price of a good softbox.

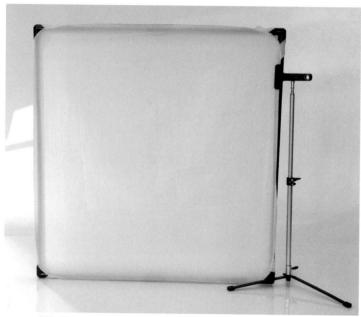

5.4 A diffusion panel

| Tip | *If you're feeling crafty, a diffusion panel can be made from items easily found in your local hardware and fabric store. Numerous sites are on the Internet that offer advice on how to construct one.* |

There are a number of low-cost devices on the market that can be used directly on the flash to provide diffusion. The Stofen Omnibounce fits directly over the flash head to diffuse the shadows. The Gary Fong Lightsphere also fits over the flash head to diffuse the light. While these devices work exceptionally well for quick shots on the go, they are no replacement for a good umbrella or softbox.

Backgrounds and Background Stands

When you want to isolate the subject, making it the sole focus of the image, use a background. Backgrounds can also be used to complement the color of an object or to accent a certain feature of the person whose portrait you are taking.

Backgrounds come in almost as many colors and materials as you can imagine. The following sections discuss some of the different types and applications.

Seamless paper backdrops

The most common types of backgrounds are made of paper. Seamless paper backdrops are inexpensive and come in every color imaginable. Standard rolls of background paper range in size from 3 feet to 12 feet wide and can be as long as 36 feet. The great thing about using paper as a background is that if it gets dirty or torn, you can cut it off and pull more down from the roll.

Starting out, getting a roll of neutral grey paper is best. You can use this color for just about any subject without worrying about the color of your subject clashing with the background. White paper is good for photographing high-key subjects, while a black background is good for photographing low-key subjects.

For more information on high key and low key, see Chapter 3.

In order to keep your portable studio manageable, sometimes it might be necessary to cut down your seamless paper backdrop. For example, when I have to travel with my portable portrait studio, I usually take a 53-inch-wide by 36 foot roll of seamless and cut it down to 48 inches wide with a hacksaw in order to make it fit into the case that holds my backdrops and stands.

5.5 A seamless paper background

Muslin backdrops

Muslin is an inexpensive lightweight cotton material. When used for backdrops, it is usually dyed different colors with a mottled pattern to give the background a look of texture. You can purchase muslin at most well-stocked photography stores or online. If you have very specific needs, there are companies that dye muslin fabric to a custom color of your choice.

 Tip *When using white, grey, or black seamless backgrounds, you can use gels on a Speedlite aimed at the backdrop to add color. A gel is a piece of colored film that you place over the light source in order to change the color. Many different companies sell these gels at reasonable prices.*

Tip *When shopping for a backdrop, consider* www.photography props.com *and* www.back dropsource.com, *both on the Web.*

Muslin is very convenient to use. It's very lightweight, it folds up easily into a small bundle, and it is pretty durable. You can drape it over your background stand or you can easily tack it to a wall. For a portable studio, this flexibility is very advantageous because the muslin doesn't take up too much valuable space when traveling.

Muslin is very versatile, and although it's much more suited to portraits, it can be used successfully for product shots as well.

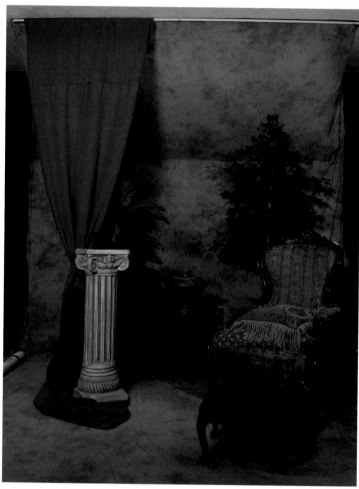

5.6 A muslin backdrop shown in a studio setting

Canvas backdrops

Canvas backdrops are very heavy duty. They are usually painted a mottled color that is lighter in the center and darkens around the edges, which helps the subject stand out from the background. These types of backdrops are almost exclusively used for portraits.

When considering a canvas backdrop, in addition to the weight factor, you should consider the cost as well – they are expensive. Although you can get them in lighter-weight smaller sizes, I wouldn't generally recommend using canvas backdrops for a portable studio as they are unwieldy and not very versatile.

Background stands

Background stands, amazingly enough, hold up your backgrounds. Most background stand kits have three pieces: two stands and a cross-bar. The cross-bar slides into a roll of paper or other backdrop and is held up by the stands. The cross-bar has two holes, one at either end, which slide over a support pin on the top of the stand. The crossbar is usually adjustable from 3 to 12½ feet, to accommodate the various widths of backdrops. The stands are adjustable in height up to 10½ feet. Most kits also come with either a carrying case or a bag for maximum portability.

There a varying degrees of quality in background stands. The more sturdy the stand, the more expensive it is. For a portable studio, a decent medium-weight background stand kit suffices.

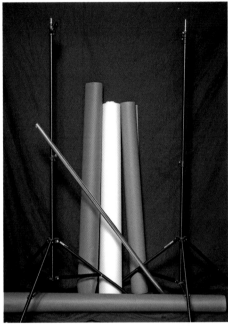

5.7 A background stand kit with carrying case

Space Requirements

Portable studios, by their very nature, don't require a lot of space to set up. As always, the more space you have, the more comfortable you are.

If your portable studio is going to be set up mostly in one place, such as a spare room in your house, then you're going to want to take measurements of the width of the space to make determinations, such as how wide your backdrop can be. Another consideration is what type of photography you plan to do. If you're going to be photographing full-length portraits, for example, the length of the room needs to be longer than if you're planning on photographing mainly head and shoulders portraits.

Setting up indoors

The first thing you want to do when setting up indoors is to find a space wide enough to accommodate your background and stands. Remember that although your backdrop may only be six feet wide, the stands extend two or three feet beyond that. Next, you want to be sure that you have enough room in front of the background to be able to move back and forth to enable you to compose your picture properly.

Depending on the type of indoor photography you are planning, your considerations differ, as the next sections explain.

Portraits

When photographing portraits, you want to use lenses with a longer focal length so you don't get the distortion that wide angle lenses often have. Unfortunately, with longer lenses comes the need for more space.

If you use a long focal length lens to photograph a head and shoulders portrait, you don't want to find your back up against the wall when you only have the head in the frame. For example, if you use an 85mm lens with a 30D, you need at least 12 feet between the camera and the subject, two or three feet behind the camera for you, and anywhere from three to six feet between the model and the background to be sure the model isn't casting shadows on the backdrop.

Be sure the area is wide enough to accommodate both the models and the lights comfortably. You want to have enough width to be able to move the lights further away from the model if needed.

When setting up to photograph portraits, you need to first decide how you want your lighting to look. Five main types of portrait lighting are

✦ **Shadowless.** This lighting is when your main light and your fill light are at equal ratios. Generally, you set up a Speedlite at 45 degrees on both sides of your model. This type of light can be very flattering although it can lack moodiness and drama.

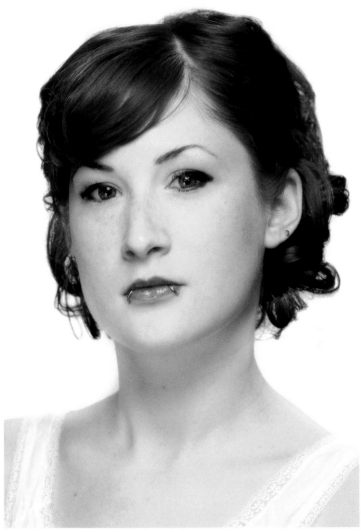

5.8 A portrait using shadowless light

✦ **Butterfly.** Also called Hollywood glamour, this type of lighting is mostly used in glamour photography. It gets its butterfly name from the shape of the shadow that the nose casts on the upper lip. You achieve this type of lighting by positioning the main light directly above and in front of your model.

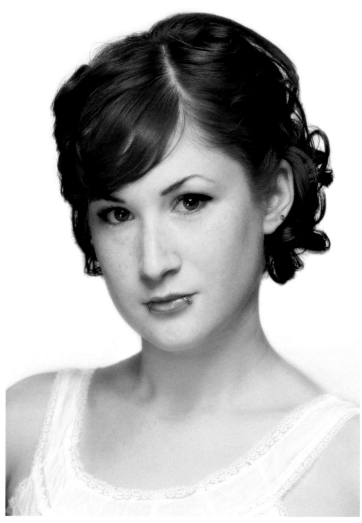

5.9 A portrait using butterfly lighting

✦ **Loop.** Also called Paramount, this is the most commonly used lighting technique for portraits. It was used so extensively by Paramount Studios in Hollywood's golden age, that this lighting pattern became synonymous with the studio's name. This lighting pattern is achieved by placing the main light at a 15-degree angle to the face making sure to keep the light high enough so that the shadow cast by the nose is at a downward angle and not horizontal.

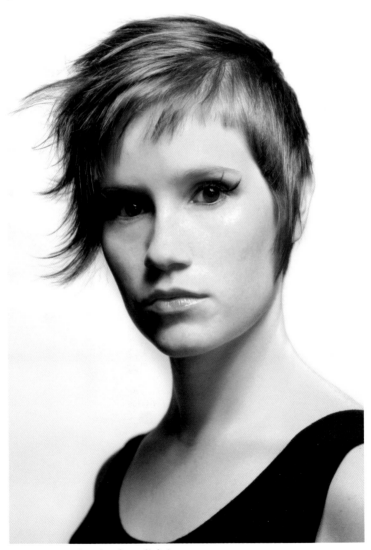

5.10 A portrait using loop lighting

✦ **Rembrandt.** This dramatic lighting pattern was used extensively by the famous artist Rembrandt van Rijn. The lighting is a moody dramatic pattern that benefits from using less fill light. The Rembrandt style is achieved by placing the light at a 45-degree angle aimed a little bit down at the subject. Again I emphasize using little or no fill light. This style is by far my favorite type of lighting.

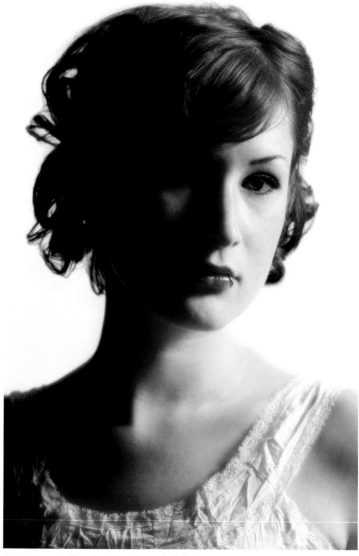

5.11 A portrait using Rembrandt lighting

✦ **Split.** This is another dramatic pattern that benefits from little or no fill. You can do this by simply placing the main light at a 90-degree angle to the model.

Small products

Photographing small products requires a lot less room than photographing people. You can move the lights much closer, and you can use a close-up or macro lens. Even

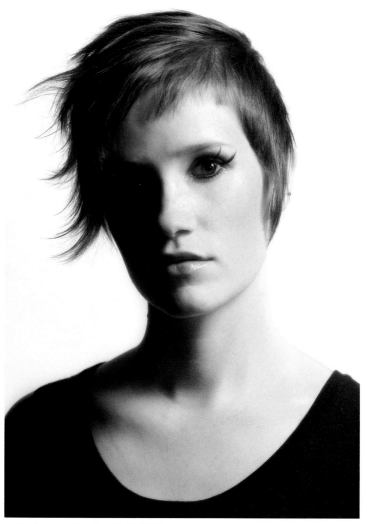

5.12 A portrait using Split lighting

when using a lens with a long focal length, you are able to be closer to the subject, thereby reducing the amount of space you need.

Using an 80-200mm lens with a 30D, you need at least six feet from the camera to the subject and two to three feet behind the camera for you. That's almost half the amount of space you need to do portraits!

The best place to start out lighting a product is to place the main light above and a little behind the product. This placing simulates a natural light, similar to sunlight, by which all lighting is judged. The next step is to note where the deep shadows are and to fill them in a bit. You do this so you can achieve detail in the shadows and not have them go completely black. You can either use a fill light or you can bounce or reflect light from the main light into the shadow areas.

Remember, a little experimentation never hurts. Move the lights around and try new and different methods.

 For more information on small product lighting see the Chapter 6 section on still life and product photography.

Setting up outdoors

The best aspect about having a portable studio is that you can take it anywhere. With the Canon Speedlite System, you can bring your lighting setup outside and not worry about having somewhere to plug in. When shooting outdoors, gone are the space restrictions you have indoors, but outdoor shooting has pitfalls all its own.

When you use your 580EX or 430EX on camera, you can use the sun as your main light, set the flash to E-TTL and shoot. If you use them off camera with stands, you need to be sure to set them on firm level ground. Also, when using a softbox or umbrella, be very conscious of the wind. The wind can take the umbrella and bring your Speedlite crashing to the ground.

When shooting outdoors you can use the same lighting situations as noted in the section on portraits, but you need to pay particular attention to the sun. Different types of sunlight have different pitfalls:

✦ **Bright sunlight.** Bright sunlight can cause serious problems with exposure when using flash. When in bright sunlight, your camera may call for a shutter speed that's higher than your camera's rated flash sync speed. You may need a higher shutter speed to achieve a proper fill flash exposure even at your smallest aperture. One way around this problem is to move your subject into a more shaded area. Canon Speedlites also offer something called High Speed Sync, which enables you to shoot at speeds higher than the actual sync speed of the camera when using an 580EX or 430EX Speedlite. This is useful if you're photographing a portrait and need to use a wider aperture for less depth of field and a very high shutter speed. The High Speed Sync mode causes the Speedlite to emit a series of lower power flashes that coincide with the movement of the shutter across the focal plane, which is where the digital sensor is. The drawback to High Speed Sync is that it diminishes the range of the Speedlite. FP High Speed Sync mode can be used all the way up the maximum shutter speed of 1/8000 second.

✦ **Cloudy bright sunlight.** This occurs when it is overcast, but you have slight shadows. This type of light is very good to photograph in. It's comparable to the light from a good softbox. All you may need to do is use your Speedlite to add a little fill-flash.

✦ **Open shade.** Open shade is defined as when your subject is in the shade but there is blue sky overhead. This situation is usually achieved by placing your subject in the shade of a building, which is a good, soft (but fairly bright) light. You can set your lighting up as you like without having to worry about too many harsh shadows from the sun.

✦ **Closed shade.** You find this type of lighting under a dense tree or under an overhang such as a veranda or porch. There aren't too many problems here caused by lighting or shadow. Set up with the lighting pattern of your choice and shoot.

Tip | *When using light stands outdoors, having sandbags placed on the stands feet to prevent the wind from blowing it over is advisable. Sandbags are commercially available through photography stores, or you can make your own.*

Cross-Reference | *Chapter 6 covers more outdoor photography tips with action and sports photography.*

Traveling with Your Wireless Studio

The first consideration you want to make when traveling with your wireless studio is getting a durable case for your equipment. Let's face it; photo gear is expensive and delicate. You don't want to stick your equipment in a suitcase and leave it to the mercy of the baggage handlers at the airport.

Camera cases and bags

A good feature about using Canon Speedlites for your portable studio is that they are compact. They fit in almost any camera bag — and there are many types of camera bags and cases from which to choose. Depending on the size and level of protection you are looking for, you may spend hundreds of dollars to as little as 20 dollars. Here are a few different types:

✦ **Pelican cases.** In my opinion, these are the best cases you can get. Pelican cases are unbreakable, watertight, airtight, dustproof, chemical-resistant, and corrosion-proof. They are built to military specs and are unconditionally guaranteed forever. Pelican cases even float in salt water with a fifty-five pound load inside. A standard Pelican case that holds two camera bodies, a wide angle to medium zoom, a telephoto zoom, and two Speedlites costs about two hundred dollars. That is not a lot of money when you consider how much it would cost to replace all of that gear if it were smashed or wet.

✦ **Shoulder bags.** These are the standard camera bags you can find at any camera shop. They come in a multitude of sizes to fit almost any amount of equipment you can carry. Reputable makers include Naneu Pro, Tamrac, and Lowepro. Look them up on the Web to peruse the various styles and sizes.

✦ **Backpacks.** You wear these camera cases on your back just like a standard backpack. These also come in different sizes and styles. Some even offer laptop carrying capabilities. The type of backpack case I use when traveling is a Naneu Pro Alpha. The design looks like a military pack, so thieves don't even know you are carrying camera equipment. When traveling, I usually pack this up with two camera bodies, a wide angle zoom, a long telephoto, three or four prime lenses, two Speedlites, a reflector disk, a twelve-inch PowerBook, and all of the plugs, batteries, and other accessories that go along with my gear. And, with all that equipment packed away, I still have space left

over for a lunch. Lowepro and Tamrac also make some very excellent backpacks.

Backgrounds and light stands

Although background stand kits and light stands are available with carrying cases, I find it easier to put everything in one case. It might sound strange, but a gun case works great for carrying two light stands, two background stands, the background cross-bar, and roll of seamless background paper that has been cut down to a smaller size. Gun cases are available at sporting good stores and are relatively inexpensive. Additionally, they come in various sizes and weights — the possibilities are endless.

The hard sides keep my equipment safe, and the cases are generally lockable so no one can get into my gear without a key. It may look a bit strange, but they are a great alternative to the soft cases many stands come with, and you can carry several items in one case.

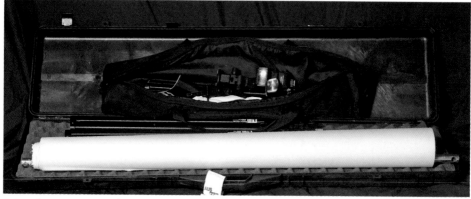

5.13 The gun case makes a great travel case for background stands and seamless backdrops. Light stands, Speedlites, and umbrellas can all be carried in the bag that the background stands originally came with.

Real-World Applications

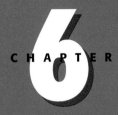
N ow that you've got the hang of using your Speedlite, it's time to put your skills to use in the real world. This chapter details many different kinds of photography and offers you insight on how to approach many subjects as well as tips and suggestions from real, professional experiences. Try the formulas and insight you gather here with your own flash photography for great results.

Action and Sports Photography

Action and sports photography is just what it sounds like, although it doesn't necessarily mean your subject is engaging in some type of sport. It can be any activity that involves fast movement, such as your child riding his bike down the street or running across the beach. Shooting any type of action can be tricky to even seasoned pros. You need to be sure to shoot at a fast enough shutter speed to freeze the movement of your subject.

When shooting with a Speedlite, you're limited to using the top sync speed that your camera allows, usually around 1/250 second, which sometimes may not be fast enough to freeze the motion. Fortunately, the flash duration is usually quick enough to freeze the motion regardless of the shutter speed. *Flash duration* is the length of time that the flash is actually lit. When using the flash in E-TTL mode while spot metering, the flash exposure is usually brighter than the ambient light therefore canceling out any chance of the ambient light reflecting off of the subject being recorded to the sensor and causing a motion blur.

You can employ a number of different techniques to further decrease motion blur on your subject. The most commonly used technique is panning. *Panning* is following the moving subject with your camera lens. With this method, it is as if the subject is not moving at all because your camera is moving with it at the same speed. When done correctly, the subject should be in sharp focus while the motion of the camera blurs the background. This effect is great for showing the illusion of motion in a still photograph too. While panning you can sometimes use a slower shutter speed to exaggerate the effect of the background blur. Panning can be a very difficult technique to master and requires a lot of practice.

> **Note** *Using flash for action/sports photography is not always necessary or advisable. Sometimes you are so far away from the action your flash won't be effective or you may be in a situation where flash is not allowed. In these cases, just make sure you have a fast enough shutter speed to freeze the motion. You can either use a lens with a wider aperture or crank up your ISO setting to be sure you get the proper shutter speed.*

Inspiration

When looking for action scenes to shoot, I tend to gravitate toward the more exciting and edgy events. On your own, just keep your eyes open; just about everywhere you look some kind of action is taking place.

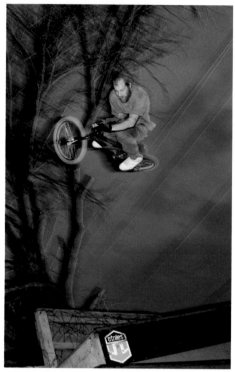

6.1 Chris Hallman, table at the T-1 ramp, Austin TX / Canon 30D with Canon 18-55 f/3.5-4.5, 1/15 sec. at f/9, evaluative metering mode with 580EX set to E-TTL

Go to the local parks and sports fields. For example, almost every weekend is a soccer tournament at the school across the street from my studio. I often go there just to practice getting action shots. Check your local newspapers for sporting events. Often the local skateboard shops and bike shops have contests. I try to take pictures of people having fun doing what they love to do.

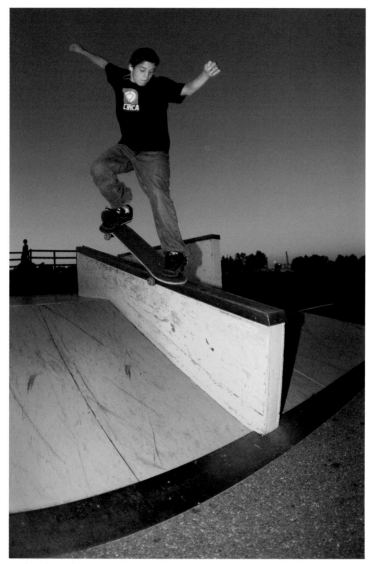

© *Photo by Anthony Armstrong — www.flickr.com/people/aarmstrong/*
6.2 Mike Bell, crook / Canon 1D with Zenitar 16mm fisheye, ISO 400, 1/1600 sec. at f/4 with 430EX set to E-TTL high-speed sync

Action and sports photography practice

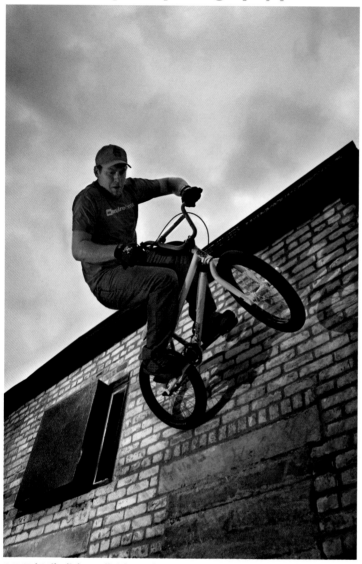

6.3 Taj Mihelich, wall ride at theT-1 Ramp, Austin, TX / Canon 30D with Canon 18-55 f/3.5-5.6, ISO 400, 1/250 sec. at f/5 with 580EX off camera fired via ST-E2 set to E-TTL evaluative metering

Table 6.1
Taking Action and Sports Pictures

Setup	**Practice Picture:** For figure 6.3, I was photographing professional BMX rider Taj Mihelich. I set up a 580EX on a lightstand to the left of the camera pointed at the wall, where I knew he would be riding.
	On Your Own: When photographing a sporting event, if at all possible, try to figure out where the action is and have your Speedlite(s) set up there.
Lighting	**Practice Picture:** The light that day was very flat since it was overcast, yet I wanted more dramatic and directional lighting. I placed the 580EX off to the side to make the lighting directional and purposely used no type of diffusion in order to cast a hard shadow on the wall and also to bring out some of the texture of the bricks.
	On Your Own: If the shot is set up, as this one was, think about what kind of effect you're looking for prior to shooting and modify (or don't) the light to suit your needs.
Lens	**Practice Picture:** I used a Canon 18-55mm set to 18mm to fit everything in the frame and to get some wide-angle perspective distortion to make the shot more interesting.
	On Your Own: Depending on how close you can get to your subject, you may want to use a telephoto lens.
Camera Settings	**Practice Picture:** My camera was set to the Action program mode to ensure that I had a fast enough shutter speed to freeze the action. Most times when shooting sports I choose Shutter Priority mode, or Action program mode, because when shooting action such as this, the aperture setting and depth of field are secondary to getting a fast shutter speed.
	On Your Own: When photographing action, setting your shutter speed is the key to capturing the image properly. Whether you want to stop motion by using a fast shutter speed or blur the background using a slower shutter speed and panning with your subject, you want to be able to control the shutter speed in Shutter Priority mode.

Continued

Table 6.1 *(continued)*

Exposure	**Practice Picture:** 1/250 at f/5, ISO 400.
	On Your Own: Try to use the fastest shutter speed you can in order to stop motion. If the light is dim, you may need to bump up your ISO, as I did for this shot, in order to lessen your flash output to avoid the Speedlite firing at full power and draining the batteries quickly.
Accessories	When using a lens with a long focal length, a monopod or tripod can help steady the camera resulting in sharper images.

Obtaining Permission

When photographing people, it's generally a good idea to ask if they mind if you take their pictures. This is especially true when photographing children. You should *always* find a parent or guardian and ask permission before photographing children.

Generally, I keep a pad and paper with me. I ask for a mailing address or e-mail address, and I offer to send them a copy of the photo, either in print form or as an electronic file.

If you're planning to publish your photographs, it's also a good idea to have a photo release form, also known as a model release, on hand. This document, when signed by the person you photographed, allows you to use the image at your discretion.

If your subject is under the age of 18, you must have the parent or legal guardian sign the release form.

Many sample photo release forms are available on the Internet. Read them carefully to choose the right one for your photography usage.

Action and sports photography tips

✦ **Scope out the area to find where the action is.** Getting a great action shot is being at the right place at the right time. Before you break out your camera and start shooting, take some time to look around to see what's going on.

✦ **Stay out of the way!** Be sure you're not getting into anybody's way. It can be dangerous for you and the person doing the activity. Also, when shooting a sporting event, don't touch the ball! While shooting a baseball tournament, a foul ball rolled to my foot and I instinctively knocked it away. It cost the team a run. The coach was NOT happy with me. Luckily, they were up 14 to 1, so it wasn't a big deal, but I'll never touch another ball again!

✦ **Practice makes perfect.** Action photography is not easy. Be prepared to shoot a lot of images. After you get comfortable with the type of event you're shooting, you'll learn to anticipate where the action will be and you'll start getting better shots.

✦ **Don't be afraid to experiment with different shutter speeds.** Sometimes slowing down the shutter speed and letting the flash freeze the action, known as "dragging" the shutter, can result in interesting effects.

Animal and Pet Photography

Photographing pets is something every pet owner likes to do. I've got enough pictures of my dog to fill a 300 gig hard drive. The most difficult aspect about pet photography is getting the animal to sit still. Whether you're doing an animal portrait or just taking some snapshots of your pet playing, your Speedlite is a handy tool.

If your pet is fairly calm and well trained, photographing it in a studio setting is entirely possible. For example, my cat, Charlie Murphy, is a pretty relaxed character who doesn't mind sitting for me on occasion.

While you might be able to entice Fluffy to sit still long enough with the promise of treats to snap a few great shots using your Speedlite, not all animals are as cooperative. If you are photographing at a zoo or pet store, the animals are likely to be less well-trained. In those cases you have to look harder for interesting opportunities — and don't necessarily rule an animal out just because it isn't warm and fuzzy.

Tip *When taking photographs of animals that are behind glass, you can set your Speedlite off to the side to avoid the glare of its reflection.*

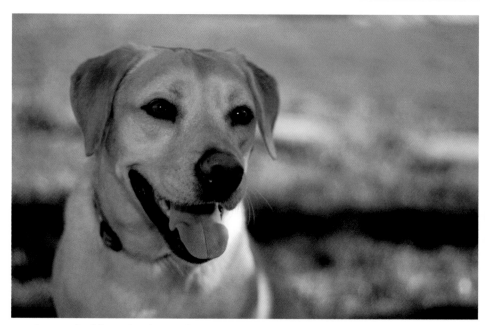

6.4 Oregon (Golden Labrador Retriever) / Canon 30D with Canon 50mm f/1.8, ISO 100, 1/2000 sec. at f/1.8, evaluative metering, 580EX set to E-TTL, FP high speed sync with a Lightsphere II to diffuse the flash

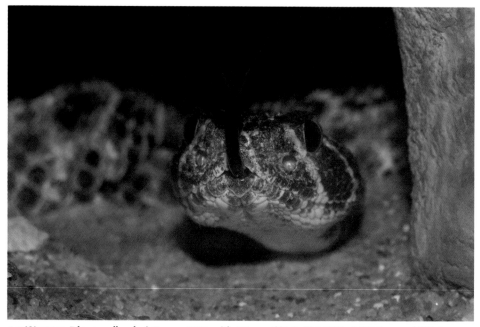

6.5 Western Diamondback / Canon 30D with 50mm f/1.8, ISO 200, 1/500 sec. at f/2.8. 430EX on Speedlite stand camera right, set to E-TTL, fired wireless with ST-E2, spot metering

Inspiration

Animals and pets are an inspiration in and of themselves. If you don't have pets yourself, go visit a friend or relative who has one. Zoos are also a good place to find unusual animals to photograph.

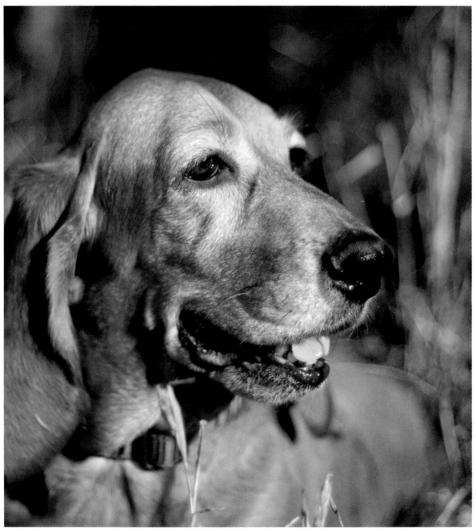

6.6 Chloe the Bassett Hound / Canon 30D with Canon 50mm f/1.8, ISO 100, 1/4000 sec. at f/1.8 evaluative metering with 430EX set to E-TTL, FP high speed sync

Animal and pet photography practice

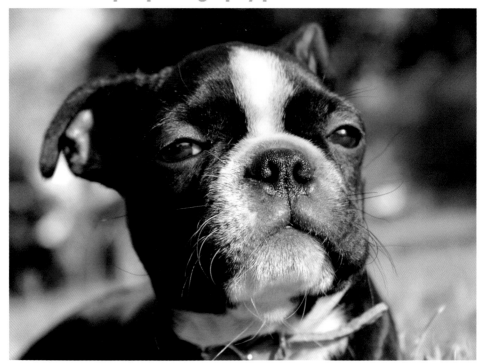

6.7 Henrietta (Boston Terrier) / Canon 30D with Canon 50mm f/1.8, ISO 400, 1/60 sec. at f/1.8 430EX on-camera E-TTL mode

Table 6.2 Taking Animal and Pet Pictures	
Setup	**Practice Picture:** In figure 6.7, I was trying for a portrait type shot that captured Henrietta's laid-back demeanor.
	On Your Own: Not all pet portraits need to be traditional and posed. Every animal has its own personality; strive to bring it out in your image.

Lighting

Practice Picture: I used a 430EX mounted on the camera set to E-TTL. Red-eye reduction on the camera body was set to On.

On Your Own: Because animals, especially dogs, are inquisitive, I find it easier to use the Speedlite mounted on the camera's hot shoe or to use the built-in Speedlite. This way I can move with the pet instead of trying to persuade it to sit in one spot. When using the Speedlite on camera, be sure to use red-eye reduction to avoid the colored reflection from your animal subject's eyes (the red-eye effect color varies in animals).

Lens

Practice Picture: For this shot I used a Canon 50mm f/1.8. This is a great all-around portrait lens. This lens in very inexpensive and very good. Its wide aperture allows you to throw the background out of focus while maintaining sharp focus on the subject.

On Your Own: Almost any lens can be used for pet photography: from standard length and telephoto to wide-angle lenses. While you don't want to photograph people's portraits with a wide-angle lens, a lot of times the perspective distortion that they give can add interest to a pets' face.

Camera Settings

Practice Picture: I set my camera to Av mode in order to control the depth of field.

On Your Own: As with portraits of humans, use a wide aperture to throw the background out of focus.

Exposure

Practice Picture: 1/250 sec. at f/2.8, ISO 100.

On Your Own: Set your shutter speed at or near your camera's sync speed.

Accessories

Try using a flash mounted softbox or diffusion dome to soften the light.

Animal and pet photography tips

✦ **Be patient!** Animals aren't always the best subjects; they can be unpredictable and uncooperative. Have patience and shoot plenty of pictures; you never know what you're going to get.

✦ **Bring some treats.** Sometimes animals can be compelled to do things with a little bribe.

✦ **Get low.** Because we're used to looking down at most animals, we tend to shoot down at them. Get down low and shoot from the animal's perspective.

✦ **Shoot wide open.** If you're at a zoo and the animal is within a cage, sometimes getting close to the cage and shooting with a wide aperture can cause the cage wire to be so far out of focus that it's hardly noticeable. Using a wide aperture can also blur out distracting elements.

✦ **Keep an eye on the background.** When photographing animals at a zoo, keep an eye out for cages and other features that look manmade — and avoid them. It's best to try to make the animal look like it's in the wild by finding an angle that shows foliage and other natural features.

Concert Photography

Doing concert photography can be both frustrating and rewarding. Sometimes to get "the" shot, you have to get in and fight a crowd, blowing your eardrums out in the process, and getting drinks spilled all over your gear. Of course, if you're the type of person who likes to get into the fray, this is great fun.

Tip | *I strongly suggest that you invest in good earplugs if you plan to do much of this type of photography.*

At larger venues, photographers usually are granted a spot up front from which to shoot, but usually these spots are reserved for pros on assignment, and getting a media pass for these events can be next to impossible. A lot of large venues won't let the fans bring cameras in, but if you are allowed, bring a telephoto lens to get close-up shots without having to get close up.

Some photographers are staunchly against using flash at concerts preferring to shoot with the available light. I for one prefer to use some flash as I find that sometimes the stage lights can oversaturate the performer resulting in the loss of detail. Another downside to shooting with available light is the high ISO settings you need to use in order to get a shutter speed fast enough to stop action. Typically you need to shoot anywhere from ISO 800 to 1600 resulting in noisy images and loss of image detail.

When photographing a band or performer, you're usually in a low-light situation. Although the stage lights are bright, they're often not as bright as you need. Even when using a Speedlite, getting a fast lens in order to capture as much light as possible is best.

Lenses with faster apertures, lenses that are f/2.8 or wider, also focus faster in low-light than do slower lens or lenses that are f/3.5 or smaller. When you use a faster lens, your flash can fire at a lower power, thereby lengthening your battery life. I also recommend setting your camera at or near ISO 400. This setting also helps keep the battery consumption down while not producing an overly noisy image.

Note *Because some venues or performers do not allow flash photography at all, just use the fastest lens available and try to use the lowest ISO you can while still maintaining a fast enough shutter speed.*

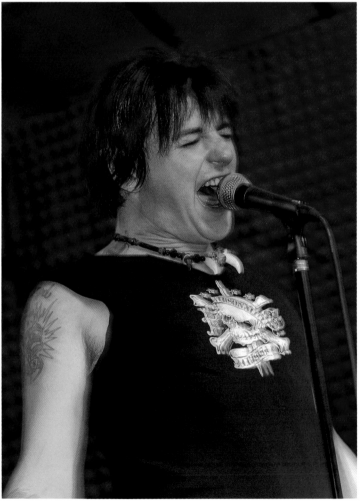

6.8 Phil Lewis of L.A. Guns at Red Eyed Fly, Austin, TX / Canon 30D with Canon 50mm f/1.8, ISO 100, 0.6 sec at f/2.8, 580EX on camera set to E-TTL, Night Portrait scene mode

Using Second Curtain Sync

Second curtain sync, also known as rear curtain sync, allows the flash to fire at the end of the exposure. When photographing moving subjects, if the flash fires at the beginning of the exposure, the ambient light being recorded causes a blur in front of the subject, which can look unnatural. Using second curtain causes the motion blur to lead up to or follow the subject. Second curtain sync is most effective when using a long shutter speed.

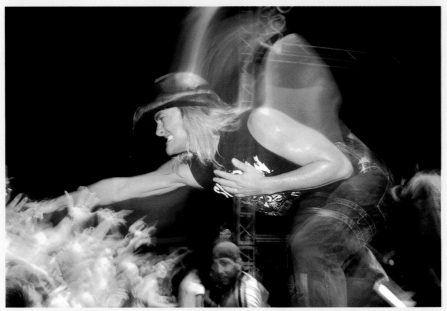

Johnny Solinger of Skid Row, Austin TX / Second curtain sync allows the motion blur to trail behind the moving subject.

Occasionally, I like to stop down my lens a bit resulting in a longer shutter speed allowing the ambient light to add some motion blur and helping to show some action. This is known as *dragging the shutter*. When the flash fires, it freezes the subject, but the ambient light is still recorded as a blur. When using this technique, it is usually best to set your flash to second curtain sync so that the motion blur is behind the subject.

When photographing bands and performers, try to make it look interesting. Get down low and shoot up at the band, or if you can, get up high and shoot down at them. Try holding your camera at different angles — not all shots have to be straight on. Making your images unconventional and compelling can be the difference between a snapshot and a truly interesting and artistic photo.

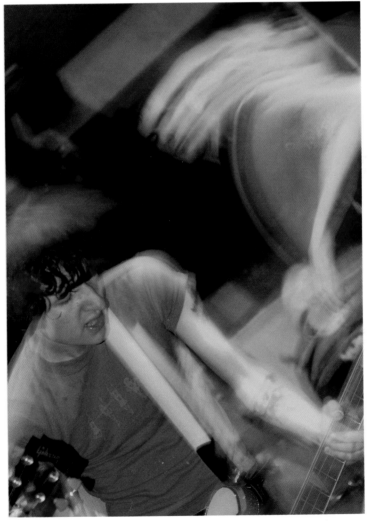

6.9 The Pink Swords at Room 710, Austin TX / Canon 30D with Canon 50mm f/1.8, ISO 400, 0.8 sec at f/2.8, 580EX on camera set to E-TTL, second curtain sync, evaluative metering

Inspiration

A good way to get your feet wet with concert photography is to find out when your favorite band or performer is playing and bring your camera. Smaller clubs are usually better places to take good close-up photos.

The key is to take pictures of what you like. Most local bands, performers, and regional touring acts don't mind having their photos taken. Offer to e-mail them some images for them to use on their Web site. This is beneficial for both them and you, as lots of people are able to see your images.

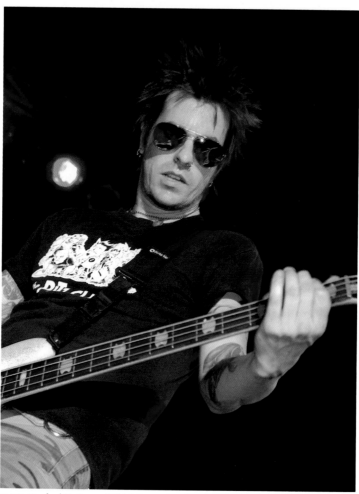

6.10 Rachel Bolan of Skid Row, Austin TX / Canon 30D with Canon 28-135mm f/3.5-5.6 set at 50mm, ISO 800, 1/80 sec. at f/4.5, 430EX hand held camera left, set to E-TTL fired wireless with ST-E2, evaluative metering

Concert photography practice

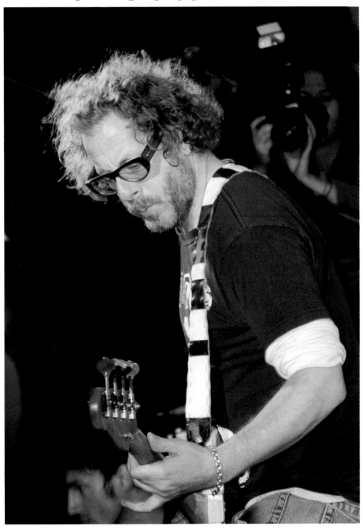

6.11 Zander Schloss, The Circle Jerks, Waterloo Park, Austin, TX / Canon 30D with Canon 28-135mm f/3.5- 5.6 set at 50mm, ISO 100, 1/8 sec. at f/4.5, 430EX set to E-TTL fired wireless with ST-E2, evaluative metering

Table 6.3
Taking Concert Pictures

Setup	**Practice Picture:** For figure 6.11, I was on the stage which although grants you greater access to the band, can be somewhat limiting because the performers are usually facing the crowd. **On Your Own:** Try to catch the performer doing something interesting rather than just standing still. Wait for the peak of the action and shoot.
Lighting	**Practice Picture:** For this image, I set my 430EX to slave mode using the ST-E2 as the master unit. I held the Speedlite high up in my left hand while pointing the flash head slightly down. **On Your Own:** Experiment with using the flash off-camera or just leave it in the camera's hot shoe.
Lens	**Practice Picture:** Canon 28-135mm f/3.5- 5.6 IS. This normal to short telephoto lens was just perfect because I wasn't very far away from the band. **On Your Own:** If you're going to be getting close to the stage, a wide-angle lens is great. The perspective distortion you get with wide-angle lenses can lend a creative look to your images. If you're going to be far from the stage a nice fast telephoto lens is advisable.
Camera Settings	**Practice Picture:** My camera was set to Aperture Priority mode. Make sure you're getting as much light to the sensor as possible. When using a flash in a low-light situation, the quick flash duration compensates for a slow shutter speed. **On Your Own:** Try to use the Aperture Priority mode in low light situations. This ensures that you don't get underexposures caused by setting your shutter speed at too high of a setting.
Exposure	**Practice Picture:** ISO 100, 1/8 sec. at f/4.5. **On Your Own:** Use as low of an ISO as you can to reduce noise. Slower shutter speeds let more ambient light in, resulting in a more colorful and interesting image.
Accessories	If you don't have an ST-E2 or 580EX to do wireless flash, you can use the SC-2 E-TTL hot shoe sync cord for off-camera flash.

Concert photography tips

✦ **Experiment.** Don't be afraid to try different settings and long exposures. Long exposures enable you to capture much of the ambient light while freezing the subject with the short bright flash.

✦ **Call the venue before you go.** Be sure to call the venue to ensure that you are able to bring your camera in. If they do allow photography, be sure to confirm that they allow your type of equipment. I've been to an event that allowed photography, but didn't allow "pro-level" equipment. The management's idea of pro-level equipment and my idea of pro-level equipment didn't quite mesh, therefore my camera gear had to be stashed in the car.

✦ **Bring earplugs.** Protect your hearing. After spending countless hours in clubs without hearing protection, my hearing is less than perfect. You don't want to lose your hearing. Trust me.

✦ **Take your Speedlite off of your camera.** Get an ST-E2 or invest in a Canon off camera shoe cord 2. When you're down in the crowd, your Speedlite is very vulnerable. The shoe-mount is not the sturdiest part of the flash. Back before wireless flash, I had a couple of Speedlites broken off at the shoe, which is unpleasant to say the least. Not only is using the Speedlite off camera safer, but also you have more control of the light direction by holding it in your hand. This reinforces the suggestion to experiment — move the Speedlite around; hold it high; hold it low; or bounce it. This is digital, and it doesn't cost a thing to experiment!

Event and Wedding Photography

Because an event is a limited occurrence, you need to be sure to capture the key moments. In a wedding, this pinnacle is usually the kiss and the cutting of the cake. For an event such as a political rally, you want to be sure to catch the keynote speaker. Events vary, so obviously, for different events you need to capture different moments.

Planning is the key to successfully photographing an event. Be sure to make a list of what you need to capture. Talk to the event planner, the bride, or the person holding the event to find out what kind of images they want. Make sure you have all the photography equipment you need for the setting, enough flash cards, and plenty of batteries for your Speedlites. That last thing you want to do is not be able to finish the job because you ran out of memory or your batteries died.

Photographing events can be very tricky. The lighting situations are varied, people are performing random acts, and you never know what may happen. You have to keep on your toes and keep an eye open for whatever interesting situations may present themselves.

Remember that not all events — especially weddings — require traditional photography. Yes, of course, you want to provide a bride and groom the array of traditional poses, but taking many shots of the in-between times can yield great images, too. For example, in figure 6.12, some of the candid, photojournalistic-style wedding shots turned out to be some of the most charming of the day.

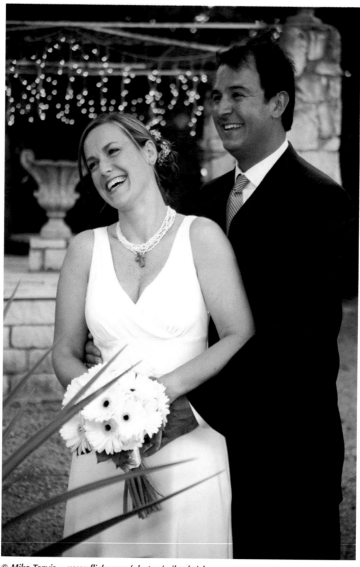

© Mike Travis – www.flickr.com/photos/mikeybrick

6.12 Wedding, Austin, TX / Canon 5D with Canon 50mm f/1.8, ISO 400, 1/30 sec. at f/5.6 with 430EX set to E-TTL

Inspiration

During a business party or wedding, try to take photos of people having fun and enjoying themselves. Catching the tone of the event is the essential job of the photographer.

Be sure to move around and take photos from different angles. Don't spend the whole event camped out in one spot. Talk to the people around you to put them at ease. Some folks are shy around cameras. You don't want to have nervous-looking people in your pictures.

At weddings, take lots of pictures of the bride and bridesmaids getting ready and the families of the bride and groom interacting. Not only does this create a great story line for the wedding pictures later, it gets the families and wedding party used to you and your equipment. Eventually, they stop posing so much and become relaxed.

At non-traditional events be sure to catch the spirit and energy of the moment. Another thing to keep in mind is you don't always have to shoot in color, many cameras offer an in-camera black & white option, or preferably the images can be changed in post processing. For example, in figure 6.13,

I converted the image to black and white to emulate the type of photography done by Glen E. Freidman in the early 80s.

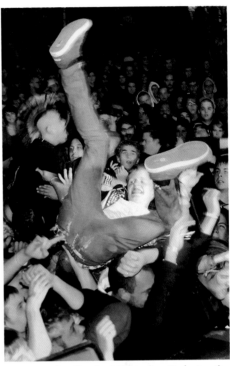

6.13 Fun fun fun fest, Waterloo Park, Austin, TX / Canon 30D with Canon 80-200mm f/2.8, ISO 800, 1/25 sec. at f/2.8 with 430EX set to E-TTL spot metering

Event and wedding photography practice

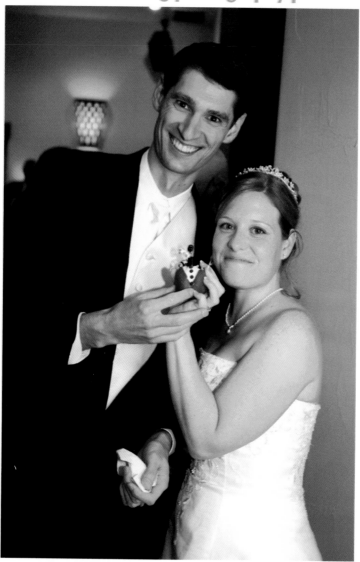

6.14 Wedding, Austin, TX / Canon 5D with Canon 17-50mm f/2.8, ISO 500, 1/30 sec. at f/5 with 580EX set to E-TTL bounced off of the wall for diffusion

Table 6.4
Taking Event and Wedding Pictures

Setup	**Practice Picture:** The couple in figure 6.14 was advised about where to stand and what to do, but they were not formally posed. **On Your Own:** Try for shots that are posed, but with a casual feel.
Lighting	**Practice Picture:** This photo was shot indoors where there wasn't much light so the Speedlite had to be the primary source of light. Shots with the flash pointed straight at the subject tend to look harsh so the flash head was pointed toward the wall and bounced. **On Your Own:** Use bounce flash or a diffuser to soften the light.
Lens	**Practice Picture:** Canon 17-50mm f/2.8. **On Your Own:** When photographing an event, having a wide assortment of focal length lenses in order to be prepared for different types of shots is a good idea.
Camera Settings	**Practice Picture:** Aperture Priority. **On Your Own:** Use Aperture Priority to control your depth of field, but be prepared to switch to Shutter Priority if the action becomes fast.
Exposure	**Practice Picture:** 1/30 sec. at f/5, ISO 500. **On Your Own:** Be sure to alter your settings to fit the event. Sometimes things slow so you can use Aperture Priority, but when the action picks up you may need to use Shutter Priority.
Accessories	When photographing events indoors you may want to use a *flash bracket*. A flash bracket connects to your camera and holds the flash high and off to the side. This prevents harsh shadows from being visible, especially when shooting indoors.

Event and wedding photography tips

✦ **Take lots of shots.** When there is a lot of movement and action going on around you at an event, you never know what you may miss if you stop shooting during a demonstration or ceremony, for example. So, you might end up with the best picture of the day just when you were ready to put your camera down.

✦ **Be prepared.** Make sure you have everything you need. Be sure you have enough memory cards for your camera and batteries for your flash.

✦ **Get there early.** If you get there early, especially with popular events, you can get some shots of the setup, preparations, and surroundings without so many people to contend with. You can also scout out locations for events that may occur during festivals, for example, so you can find the best location to get your photos.

✦ **Be aware.** You want to catch anything interesting or pertinent to the event, so keep your eyes open.

Environmental Portrait Photography

Environmental portraits show people in their environment, which isn't necessarily in an outside setting. A typical environmental portrait may show the CEO of a corporation with his factory in the background, an author in his study, or a farmer in his field.

The best way to decide what environment to photograph your subject in is to get to know the person. Talk to your subjects to find out what they do for living or what their hobbies are. If possible, visit places of employment, worksites, and other pertinent locations to look for suitable backgrounds.

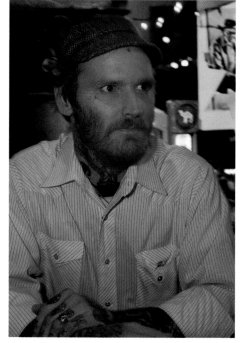

6.15 Shawn, Bartender, Long Branch Inn, Austin TX / Canon 30D with Canon 18-55 f/3.5-4.5, ISO 400, 0.3 sec at f/5 430EX ETTL slow sync with Lightsphere for diffusion

Inspiration

Find people with interesting lines of work, such as a chef, and photograph him in his kitchen. Maybe photograph a welder or an artist standing near his or her latest piece. You can find something interesting in almost any line of work. You can also photograph someone who has an interesting hobby.

Once again, talk to the person; he or she probably has some ideas for interesting settings as well. After all, your subject knows better than anyone what the most interesting part of his or her job is.

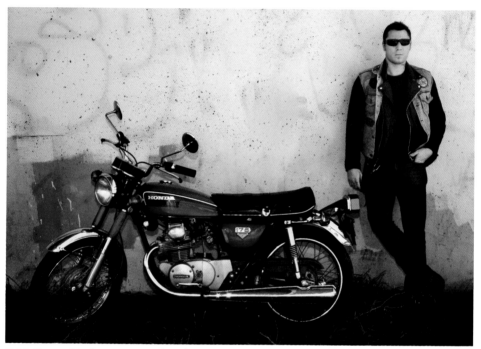

6.16 Denny Mack at Lower Colorado River, Austin TX / Canon 30D with Canon 28-135mm f/3.5-5.6 set at 28mm, ISO 200, 1/30 sec. at f/20, 430EX on stand camera left, bounced from umbrella; 580EX on stand camera right, bounced from umbrella; ST-E2 set to E-TTL ratio 1:1

Environmental portrait photography practice

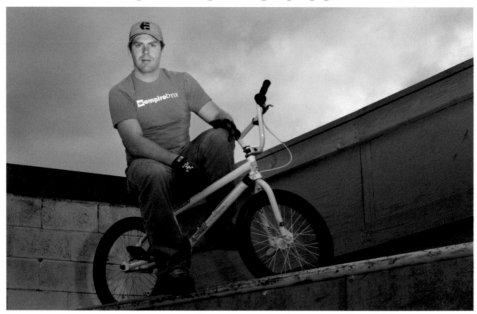

6.17 Taj Mihelich of Terrible One, Austin, TX / Canon 30D with Canon 18-55mm f/3.5-4.5 – 50mm, ISO 320, 1/250 sec. at f/5.6 with 580EX set to E-TTL

Table 6.5
Taking Environmental Portrait Pictures

Setup	**Practice Picture:** Figure 6.17 photo shows Taj Mihelich, professional BMX rider and co-owner of Terrible One, a BMX bike manufacturing company. What better way to show him than on his bike at the ramp behind his office.
	On Your Own: When photographing environmental portraits try to show some of what the subject and the subject's interest are about – strive to put some of your subject's personality in the portrait.

Lighting	**Practice Picture:** I used a 580EX on a lightstand to the right of Taj on the deck of the ramp. I was on the ground so I used the ST-E2 set to E-TTL to fire the 580EX wirelessly. **On Your Own:** Use the flash wirelessly in order to get the lighting pattern you desire on your subject.
Lens	**Practice Picture:** Canon 18-55mm f/3.5-5.6 set to 50mm. **On Your Own:** Use a long focal length lens to flatten your model's features — the farther you are away from the model, the less the apparent distance from their features is. *Apparent distance* is the perceived distance things look from each other from a certain perspective. Be careful if you need to use a wide-angle lens because when used at a close range, it can cause noses to look big and ears to look small, especially when at close distances.
Camera Settings	**Practice Picture:** Manual exposure setting, evaluative metering. **On Your Own:** Use the Manual or Aperture Priority settings to be able to set your aperture and control your depth of field. Evaluative metering enables you to use E-TTL as a fill-flash, while spot metering sets the Speedlite to ETTL, which results in an overall brighter lighting pattern on your subject.
Exposure	**Practice Picture:** 1/250 sec. at f/5.6, ISO 320. **On Your Own:** Unless you need a slower shutter speed to convey some motion or action, using a shutter speed at or near the sync speed of your camera is generally advisable. Anywhere between 1/60 and 1/250 is sufficient. See your camera owner's manual for the top sync speed of your camera.
Accessories	You may want to diffuse the light from the Speedlite by bouncing from an umbrella or using a softbox.

Environmental portrait photography tips

✦ **Be unconventional.** Sometimes trying something out of the ordinary can really bring out your subject's personality. Think outside of the typical poses and locations. Ask to see what the subject's work involves so you can look for interesting locations or backgrounds.

✦ **Meet with your subject first.** Meet up with subjects you're photographing and talk with them about their work or hobby to get a feel for who they are. Discuss with subjects what they would like to see in the portrait; they might have some great ideas that you hadn't thought of.

✦ **Use a shorter focal length.** If you generally use a medium telephoto lens for portraits, try a shorter focal length lens instead. If you choose a wide-angle lens, don't get too close to your subject or his or her facial features may become distorted in your finished image.

✦ **Take breaks.** Giving subjects a chance to take a break allows them the opportunity to go about their work or play, which gives you the opportunity to take some shots with the subjects more at ease.

Group Photography

Group photography is basically taking pictures of multiple people, ranging from couples to entire companies. With more subjects comes more responsibility. Now, instead of having to pose one person, you have to pose multiple people. Added to that is the challenge of managing people blinking, yawning, turning their heads, and a myriad of other details.

Posing groups in attractive formations is very important — try to stay away from having them stand all in a row. Ideally, you want to position them to create a flowing pattern. Geometric patterns, such as a diamond shape, also work well when shooting four or more people.

Depending on the circumstances and location, you may want to have a few chairs or stools handy so you can have a couple people standing behind the people that are seated.

Before you are ready to begin taking shots, make sure that you have everyone's attention. You can fire a test flash, use a whistle, or any other obvious action or noise that will garner attention. This should help to settle everyone down and let them know you're about to snap the photo, which hopefully minimizes any unwanted actions by the subjects.

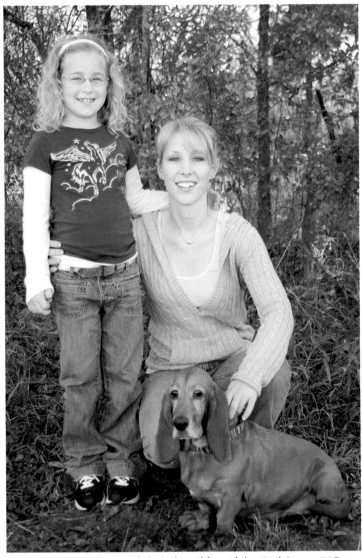

6.18 Diana and J'ana, and their dog Chloe, Elgin, TX / Canon 30D with Canon 28-135mm f/3.5-5.6 IS, ISO 400, 1/2 sec. at f/4, evaluative metering with 430EX set to E-TTL, slow sync, Lightsphere II to diffuse the flash

Inspiration

Family reunions and friendly get-togethers are good places to start taking group portraits. You can find subjects at pretty much any gathering with a lot of people. Parties, nightclubs, and social events can also be great places to photograph portraits of friends, couples, and families. And, not all portraits need to be formal; sometimes capturing the spirit of the moment or gathering is as important.

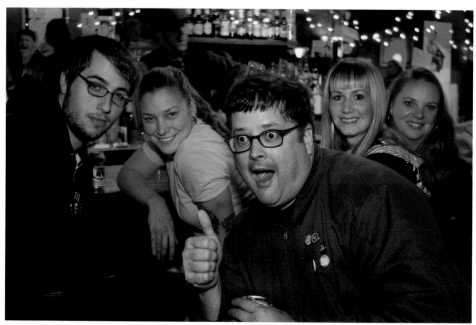

6.19 The Obsolete Industries crew, Austin, TX / Canon 30D with Canon 17-55mm f/3.5-4.5, ISO 400, 1/500 sec. at f/5.6, evaluative metering with 430EX set to E-TTL, FP high speed sync, Lightsphere II to diffuse the flash

Group photography practice

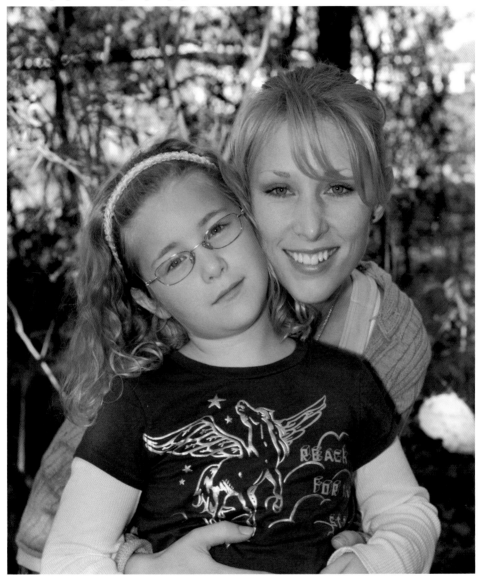

6.20 Diana and J'ana, Elgin, TX / Canon 30D with Canon 28-135mm f/3.5-5.6 IS, ISO 400, 1/500 sec. at f/5.6, evaluative metering with 430EX set to E-TTL, FP high speed sync, Lightsphere II to diffuse the flash

Table 6.6
Taking Group Pictures

Setup	**Practice Picture:** Figure 6.20 is a photograph I shot of my sister and my niece. We took the shot in a wooded area near the house to add a pleasing backdrop and to get under some shade as the sun was very bright. **On Your Own:** You can use any number of friends or relatives to achieve an effective group shot. Try to get practice in a variety of locations and with a varying number of subjects in your shots.
Lighting	**Practice Picture:** Because we were so close, I opted to use a 430EX mounted on my camera's hot shoe. I used a Gary Fong Lightsphere II to help diffuse the light to avoid any harsh shadows. **On Your Own:** Depending on how large the group is and how far away you need to be from your subjects, you may need to use more than one Speedlite. For larger groups, you need more coverage, and setting up two Speedlites on either side of you is ideal.
Lens	**Practice Picture:** Because I was pretty close and this was a small group, I used a normal to telephoto zoom lens. I had the lens zoomed to about 50mm. **On Your Own:** Group portraits usually call for a semi-wide-angle or wide-angle lens to fit more people into the frame.
Camera Settings	**Practice Picture:** The camera was set to Aperture Priority so I could control the depth of field. I wanted to use a fairly wide aperture to throw the background out of focus while making sure both of my subjects remained in sharp focus. The camera's meter was set for evaluative metering so that the 430EX would provide fill flash. **On Your Own:** Use the Manual or Aperture Priority settings to be able to set your aperture and control your depth of field. Evaluative metering lets the flash provide fill, while spot metering allows the Speedlite to provide most of the light for the subject.

Exposure	**Practice Picture:** 1/500 sec. at f/5.6, ISO 400.
	On Your Own: Use a lower ISO to reduce noise, and a wide aperture for shallow depth of field. You can use a shutter speed at or near the sync speed of your camera.
Accessories	You may want to use an umbrella or diffuser to soften the light.

Group photography tips

✦ **Watch for cover-ups.** Before you release the shutter, be sure that no one is covering up someone else.

✦ **Get everyone's attention.** When you're about to snap the photo, let everyone know — don't surprise them or you'll end up with closed eyes and turned heads. Tell them to look at the camera. If everybody knows you're about to shoot, you have better chance at catching them with eyes open and looking directly at the camera.

✦ **Take more than one shot.** Take multiple shots to ensure that you have everyone looking in the same direction, not blinking, with hands down, and so forth.

✦ **Bring an assistant.** An assistant can help you keep everyone in their place and paying attention. They can also come in handy by carrying equipment.

Macro and Close-up Photography

Macro and close-up are easily some of my favorite types of photography. Sometimes you can take the most mundane object and give it a completely different perspective just by moving in close. Ordinary objects can become alien landscapes. Insects take on a new personality when you can see the strange details of their face.

Technically macro photography can be difficult. Because the closer you get to an object, the less depth of field you get, and it can be difficult to maintain focus. When your lens is less than an inch from the face of a bug, just

breathing in is sometimes enough to lose focus on the area that you want to capture. For this reason, you usually want to use the smallest aperture your camera can handle and still maintain focus. I say usually, because a shallow depth of field can also be very useful in bringing attention to a specific detail.

When using flash for macro photography, you want to get the flash as close to the axis of your lens as possible. You do this in an effort to achieve good, strong, flat lighting, which results in maximum detail. For this reason, Canon has created a Speedlite setup designed especially for macro and close-up photography. This kit places special Speedlites directly on the end of the lens using a special adapter.

Taking into consideration that most people delve into photography as a hobby and don't have a real need to purchase the dedicated macro lighting kit, I focus on some techniques for using the 430EX or 580EX for macro and close-up techniques, rather than with the kits.

While it is possible to use a Speedlite for macro photography while mounted on the camera, it doesn't always work. The 580EX is a little better suited for doing macro work with the flash on camera as the 580EX flash head and be tilted down to -7°. When shooting extremely close up, the lens may obscure the light from the flash resulting in a dark area on the bottom of the images.

In order to get the flash on-axis and closer to the subject when shooting insects or other small live creatures, I use the flash in the wireless remote setting, and handhold it next to the front of the lens. I hold the Speedlite to the left of the lens (because my right hand is holding the camera). I generally angle the flash toward the subject. I sometimes hold the flash near the top of lens to achieve an overhead lighting effect.

When photographing still objects, I set up multiple Speedlites using the supplied stands. I place two Speedlites angled at approximately 45 degrees. Depending on how I want the image to look, I either use both of the Speedlites at their ETTL settings for even lighting or I use the ratio setting on

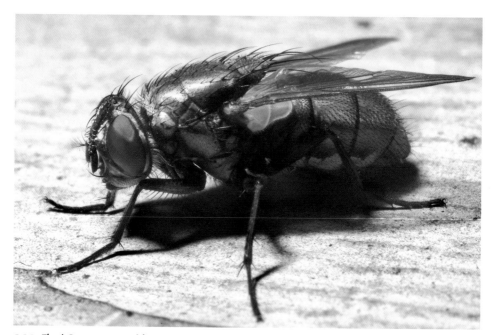

6.21 Fly / Canon 30D with Macro-Takumar 50mm f/4, ISO 200, 1/60 sec. at f/8. 580EX set to E-TTL spot metering

the Master flash or ST-E2 to get a more dramatic effect.

When shooting with the Speedlite very close to the subject, I use the built-in diffuser to soften the shadows a bit. Your Speedlite shows that the power zoom level is set to 14mm, but being so close to your subject, you don't need to worry about any light fall off. You can also use bounce flash to soften the light, but I generally don't, preferring to get the most light of out of my Speedlite in order to maintain a deep depth of field.

You may want to purchase a diffusion dome to help soften the light. Stofen makes an inexpensive one that works very well.

 Cross-Reference *For more information on alternatives to softboxes and accessories to use for portraits outside of the studio, see Chapter 5.*

Inspiration

My favorite subjects for macro photography are insects. I go to parks and wander around keeping my eyes open for strange bugs. Parks are also a great place to take macro pictures of flowers. Although bugs and flowers are the most common macro subjects, by no means are they the only subjects you can take pictures of. Lots of normal objects can become interesting when viewed up close.

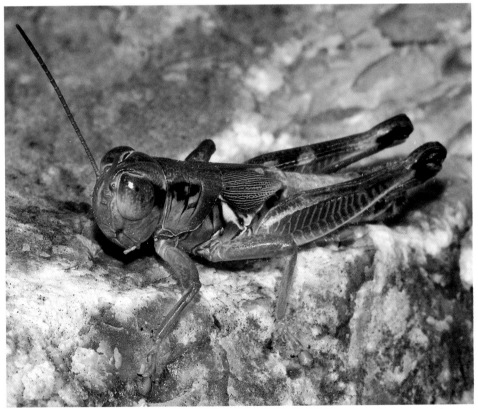

6.22 Grasshopper, Big Bend National Park, TX / Canon 30D with 50mm f/4 Macro-Takumar, ISO 200, 1/160 sec. at f/11, 580EX on camera flashhead at -7° E-TTL spot meter FEC +1

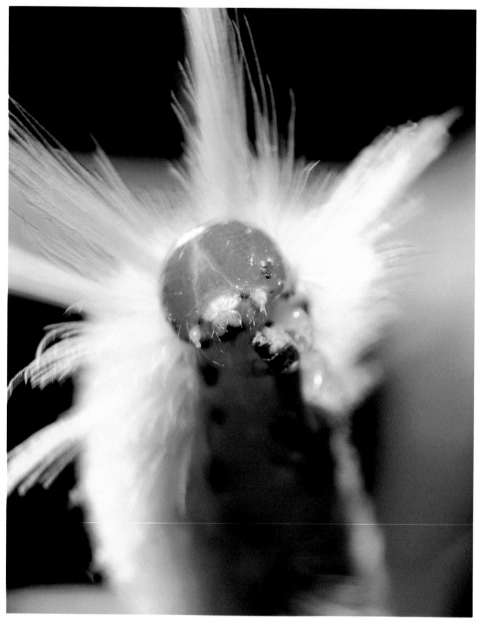

6.23 Caterpillar / Canon 30D with Macro-Takumar 50mm f/4, ISO 100, 1/125 sec. at f/8, evaluative metering with the 580EX set to ETTL fired wirelessly via ST-E2

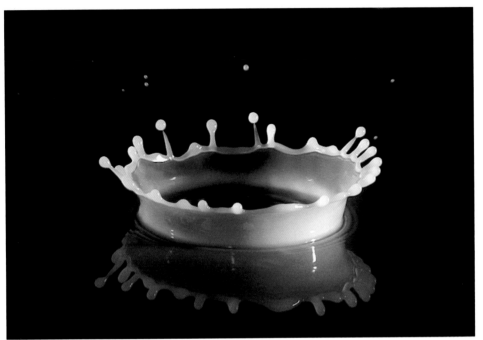

6.24 Milk drop / Canon 30D with Canon 80-200mm f/2.8, ISO 200, 1/500 sec. at f/20 with two 580EXs fired via ST-E2 set to E-TTL ratio 1:1

True Macro

Most real macro lenses are in the 50 to 60mm focal length range. True macro work is done at 1:1 perspective ratio, with the image recorded on the film or sensor being the exact same size as the actual subject. The longer focal length lenses that claim to be macro are usually 1:2, or about half size. Although they claim to be macro, they are not — they allow the illusion of macro via telephoto. Canon's higher-end telephoto macro lenses are a true 1:1.

Macro and close-up photography practice

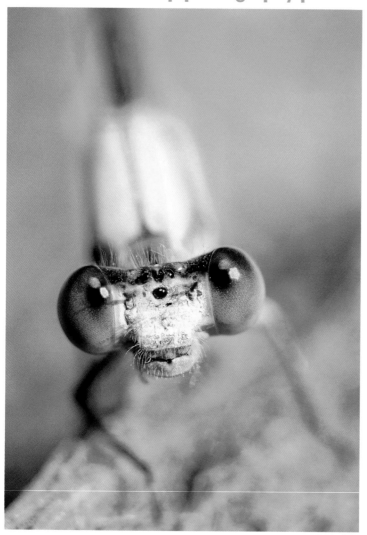

6.25 Dragonfly at the Lower Colorado River, Austin, TX / Canon 30D with Macro-Takumar 50mm f/4, ISO 100, 1/250 sec. at f/5.6, evaluative metering, with the 580EX in the camera's hot shoe set to E-TTL

Table 6.7
Taking Macro and Close-up Pictures

Setup	**Practice Picture:** Figure 6.25 is a crazy-looking dragonfly I found perched on a mossy rock on the banks of the Lower Colorado River. **On Your Own:** Look for subjects with bright colors and interesting texture, whether they are insects, flowers, or everyday objects.
Lighting	**Practice Picture:** For this shot I used a 580EX in the camera's hot shoe. The flash head was tilted down to -7°. The Speedlite was set to E-TTL. **On Your Own:** When photographing a subject such as this, you want the light a little off axis, in other words angled off to the side, in order to highlight the texture.
Lens	**Practice Picture:** 50mm Macro-Takumar f/4. (I found this lens on eBay very cheaply; it was made for old Pentax film cameras with a screw-mount.) It is manual focus, but when you're down really close to a subject, focusing is more or less achieved by moving the camera back and forth rather than focusing with the lens itself. **On Your Own:** You have many different types of macro lenses from which to choose. Longer telephoto lenses let you zoom in on the subject without actually being close. Most good macro lenses are in the 50-to-60mm range (even Canon's 100 macro and 185 macro aren't too bad) allowing a closer focus and better magnification, but resulting in less depth of field.
Camera Settings	**Practice Picture:** The camera was set to Aperture Priority mode. Most macro subjects aren't going to move at great speeds so a fast shutter speed is not really needed. Controlling the depth of field and what is in focus is more important. The camera meter was set to Evaluative to allow the Speedlite to provide fill flash. **On Your Own:** Set to Aperture Priority mode in order to have more control over the depth of field.
Exposure	**Practice Picture:** ISO 100, 1/250 sec. at f/5.6. **On Your Own:** Decide what's important in the image and focus on it. Use a relatively wide aperture to throw the background out of focus, but use a small enough aperture to maintain enough focus on the subject.
Accessories	If your subject is stationary, a tripod can be an invaluable tool.

Macro and close-up photography tips

✦ **Use close-up filters.** Close-up filters are like magnifying glasses for your lenses. If you can't afford a macro lens or you're not sure if you'd use one enough to justify the expense, these filters may be the way to go. They screw directly on the front of your lens just like any other filter and can be screwed together in order to increase the magnification more. They work fairly well and are usually priced in the thirty-dollar range. Using close-up filters can soften your image a little especially when using more than one at a time.

✦ **Try extension tubes.** Adding extension tubes enables you to get a closer focus distance with your lenses. For many, this is a less-expensive alternative to purchasing a dedicated macro lens. Extension tubes mount on your camera body in between the camera and the lens, an extension ring allows you to get closer to the subject by moving the lens forward thereby changing the *focal range* or the focusing distance of the lens.

✦ **Consider reversing rings.** These attachments allow you to attach the lens to your camera backward, which means you can focus extremely closely. Think this won't work? Have you ever looked into the wrong end of a pair of binoculars? Flipping the camera lens around works the same way.

Nature and Wildlife Photography

Photographing wildlife is a fun and rewarding pastime that can also be intensely frustrating. If you know what you want to photograph it can mean standing out in the freezing cold or blazing heat for hours on end, waiting for the right animal to show up. But when you get that one shot you've been waiting for, it's well worth it.

Wildlife photography is another one of those areas of photography where people's opinions differ on whether or not you should use flash. I tend not to use flash very often to avoid scaring off the animals. But, as with any type of photography, there are circumstances in which you might want to use a flash, such as if the animal is backlit and you want some fill-flash.

 Caution *When photographing animals in the wild, be careful! Wild animals can be unpredictable and aggressive when cornered. Give them their space and try not to disrupt the animal's routine.*

When taking nature photos, use a Speedlite to even out harsh shadows or bring detail to darker areas. By diffusing the light, your colors stay even and as crisp as you remember them to be.

Opportunities to take wildlife pictures can occur when you're out hiking in the wilderness or maybe when you're sitting out on your back porch enjoying the sunset.

With a little perseverance and luck you can get some great wildlife images just like the ones you see in *National Geographic*.

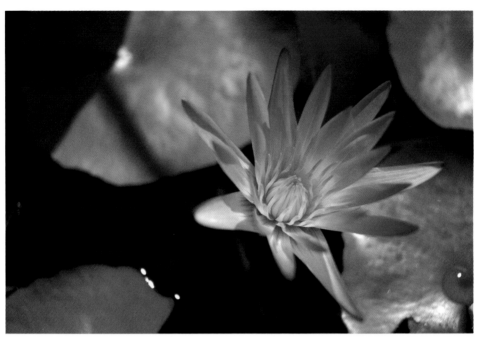

6.26 Lotus, Zilker Park Botanical Gardens, Austin, TX / Canon 30D with Canon 28mm f/2.8, ISO 200, 1/4000 sec. at f/2.8, 580EX on camera set to E-TTL FP high speed sync, spot metering

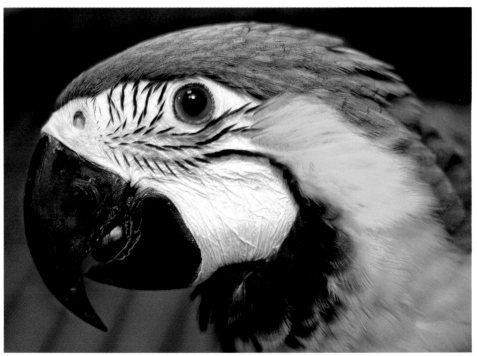

6.27 Parrot, Austin, TX / Canon 30D with Canon 50mm f/1.8, ISO 100, 1/15 sec. at f/1.8 with the 430EX set to E-TTL with a Lightsphere for diffusion, spot metered

Inspiration

You can go to wildlife reserves, a zoo, or even your backyard to find "wildlife." I tend to go the easy route, going to places where I'm pretty sure to find what I'm looking for.

For example, while driving through Louisiana recently, I saw a sign that advertised for an alligator swamp tour. I was pretty sure I'd see some alligators if I went. And even though I'd missed the last tour, there were still plenty of alligators there.

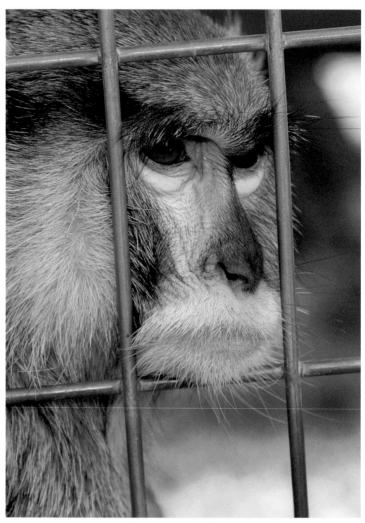

6.28 Monkey, Austin TX / Canon 30D with Canon 28-135mm f/3.5-5.6, ISO 400, 1/200 sec. at f/5.6 with the 430EX on camera set to E-TTL, evaluative metering

Even in the city or urban areas you may be able to find wildlife, such as birds perched on a power line or pigeons gathered, or even ducks and geese. A lot of cities have larger parks where you can find squirrels or other smaller animals. I'm fortunate in that there is a park near my studio where I can see peacocks and armadillos running around.

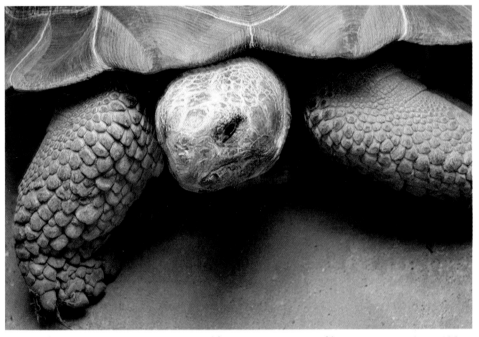

6.29 Galapagos tortoise / Canon 30D with Canon 28-135mm f/3.5-5.6 set at 65mm, ISO 400, 1/30 sec. at f/5; 580EX on camera set to E-TTL with Lightsphere for diffusion; FEC +2; evaluative metering

Nature and wildlife photography practice

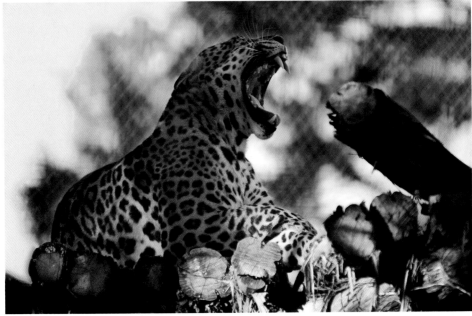

6.30 Leopard, Austin, TX / Canon 30D with Canon 80-200mm f/2.8L, ISO 100, 1/125 sec. at f/2.8 spot metered with the 430EX on the camera hot shoe set to E-TTL, FEC +2

Table 6.8
Taking Nature and Wildlife Pictures

Setup	**Practice Picture:** For figure 6.30, I noticed this leopard lounging in the sun at the zoo and decided to snap a few shots. I managed to catch him mid-yawn.
	On Your Own: Wild animals are generally pretty skittish (they are called "wild" for a reason) so moving slowly and trying not to make any loud noises is best.
Lighting	**Practice Picture:** Because the leopard was pretty far away and I couldn't get any closer, I adjusted the flash exposure compensation to +2 stops.
	On Your Own: I recommend setting the flash to E-TTL; the less you have to think about when trying not to scare an animal off, the better.

Lens	**Practice Picture:** For this shot I used a Canon 80-200 f/2.8L at 200mm zoom. I used this telephoto lens in order to get a close-up of the Leopard. Because I had to shoot through a fence I needed to use a wide aperture to allow a very shallow depth of field so the wires of the fence were sufficiently out of focus so as to be nearly invisible.
	On Your Own: Longer focal length lenses are usually recommended for shooting wildlife. Long lenses help you get close-up shots without disturbing the animal. Lens with a wider aperture can sometimes allow you to shoot through fences and bars without seeing them in the image.
Camera Settings	**Practice Picture:** Aperture Priority mode.
	On Your Own: Shutter or Aperture Priority mode. You want to use Tv mode to choose a fast enough shutter speed to freeze the motion of the animal in case it's moving. If the animal isn't moving or is behind a cage use Av mode to choose a wide aperture.
Exposure	**Practice Picture:** 1/125 sec. f/2.8 ISO 100.
	On Your Own: Depending on how fast the animal is moving and how much light you have, you may need to adjust your ISO to achieve a faster shutter speed.
Accessories	A monopod can help you hold your camera steady when photographing animals at long focal lengths.

Nature and wildlife photography tips

✦ **Use a long lens.** Whenever possible, use a long telephoto lens. This allows you to remain inconspicuous to the animal, enabling you to catch it acting naturally.

✦ **Seize an opportunity.** Even if you don't have the "right" lens on your camera for capturing wildlife, snap a few shots anyhow. You can always crop it later, if it isn't perfect. It's better to get the shot than not.

✦ **Adjust your flash exposure compensation when using a long lens.** The 430EX and 580EX zoom range only goes up to 105mm. This doesn't mean you can't use it with a lens longer than that. Adjusting the flash exposure compensation up can get more range out of your Speedlite. Of course, you may experience slower recycling times and shorter battery life.

✦ **Be patient.** It may take a few hours, or even a few trips, to the outdoors before you have the chance to see any wild animals. Keep the faith, it will happen eventually.

Night Portrait Photography

When photographing a portrait at night, remember that while the Speedlite is used to illuminate your subject, it is not enough to illuminate the background. In order to get enough light to allow the background to be properly exposed, you need to use a longer shutter speed. Consumer-level cameras, such as the Digital Rebel XT and the 30D have a Night Portrait setting that adjusts the camera's settings in order to achieve a longer shutter speed than would normally be used when using flash. This can also be accomplished manually by setting the camera to Slow Sync mode. Slow Sync mode enables you to set a slower shutter speed when the Speedlite is attached to the camera.

When using the Speedlite in Slow Sync mode to shoot night portraits, using a tripod is almost always necessary in order to reduce the blur that is caused by handholding the camera at slow shutter speeds. Fortunately, the flash from the Speedlite is quick enough

and bright enough to freeze the main subject, and so long as they don't move too much, they stay in focus with or without the tripod.

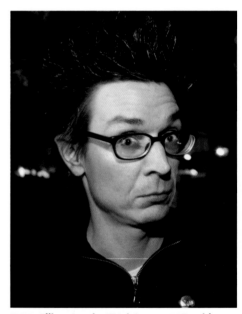

6.31 Elliot, Austin, TX / Canon 30D with Canon 28-135mm f/3.5-5.6 set to 28mm, ISO 500, 1/5 sec. at f/4.5 with the 430EX on camera set to E-TTL, evaluative metering

Inspiration

Going to areas where there's a lot of nightlife can be a great place to find people to pose for portraits for you. Look for people having fun and enjoying themselves. I've never been turned down when asking someone if I could take his or her picture. Bring a pad and pencil to get an e-mail address and offer to send them a copy of the image.

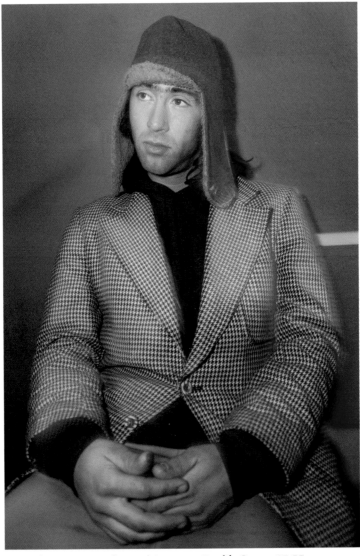

6.32 The Carny, Austin, TX / Canon 30D with Canon 17-55mm f/3.5-4.5 set to 18mm, ISO 400, 1.5 sec. at f/3.5 with the 430EX on camera set to E-TTL slow sync, evaluative metering Lightsphere for diffusion

Night portrait photography practice

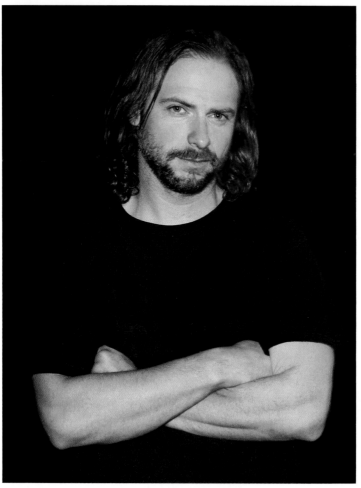

6.33 Chris at Secret Hideout Studios, Austin TX / Canon 30D with Canon 17-55mm f/3.5-5.6 set at 34mm, ISO 800, 1/4 sec. at f/5.6, 580EX on camera in Night Portrait scene mode

Table 6.9
Taking Night Portraits

Setup	**Practice Picture:** For figure 6.33, I wanted to allow some of the ambient light to add a little extra warmth to the image. I used an extra long shutter speed to ensure that the ambient light would show through. **On Your Own:** Decide how you want the image to look before shooting and be sure to set your camera to adequately capture the image.
Lighting	**Practice Picture:** 430EX mounted in the camera hot shoe. Speedlite set to ETTL with a Lightsphere for diffusion. **On Your Own:** For taking portraits at night, the Speedlite can be mounted on the camera or used off camera. When using a long shutter speed, the ambient light can soften the light from the flash allowing it to look less like a direct flash.
Lens	**Practice Picture:** Canon 17-55mm f/3.5-4.5, 34mm setting. **On Your Own:** When doing portraits you usually don't want to use a wide-angle lens due to the facial distortion it can cause. With the 1.5 crop factor of the 30D, the 34mm setting is closer to that of a normal lens on a film camera; it works out to a 52mm lens.
Camera Settings	**Practice Picture:** Night Portrait scene mode. **On Your Own:** Use the Night Portrait setting, or use the Shutter Priority mode in order to set the shutter speed slow enough to capture the ambient light.
Exposure	**Practice Picture:** 1/4 sec. at f/5.6, ISO 800. **On Your Own:** Use a long enough shutter speed for the amount of light you want to let in. In this example the shutter speed was extra long, but for a more traditional look the shutter can be set a little faster — .5 sec. will do.
Accessories	When using long shutter speeds, a tripod helps your subject stay in focus.

Night portrait photography tips

✦ **Bring a tripod.** A tripod helps keep the camera steady for the long exposures.

✦ **Use a higher ISO.** A high ISO helps keeps the shutter speed a little faster so your subject won't be blurry.

✦ **Find an interesting background.** Look for background with some brightly colored lights to add to the ambience of the image.

Outdoor Portrait Photography

Creating portraits outdoors can mean photographing your subject anywhere from a backyard, to a park, or even a jungle. Anywhere you take portrait shots that is outdoors qualifies as an outdoor portrait.

The main difference between outdoor portraits and portraits taken indoors and in studios is the use of lighting. For an outdoor portrait taken during the day, the sun, being the brightest light source is used as your key light. Your Speedlite is used to fill in the sometimes harsh shadows created by the bright sun.

I find the best way to use the Speedlite for outdoor portraits is to set it to the E-TTL setting using the evaluative metering. The camera meter takes a reading of the overall brightness of the scene and uses this reading to provide just enough light from the flash to fill in the shadows without looking like flash was used.

When shooting outdoors, paying close attention to the way the light is falling on your subject is important. Finding a location that has good lighting and makes an attractive background is the key to a successful outdoor portrait.

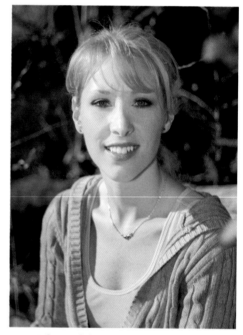

6.34 Diana, Elgin, TX / Canon 30D with Canon 50mm f/1.8, ISO 100, evaluative metering, 1/3200 sec. at f/1.8 with the 430EX set to E-TTL, diffusion dome for added softness

Inspiration

Look for areas that create interesting patterns for the background. Foliage and flowers can create nice patterns and add a splash of color. Using the beauty of nature for your backdrop can create an interesting portrait.

Placing your subject in the shade of tree or building softens the light from the sun, making the lighting more even, creating a more pleasant portrait. This setting also keeps the sun out of your models' eyes so that they aren't squinting.

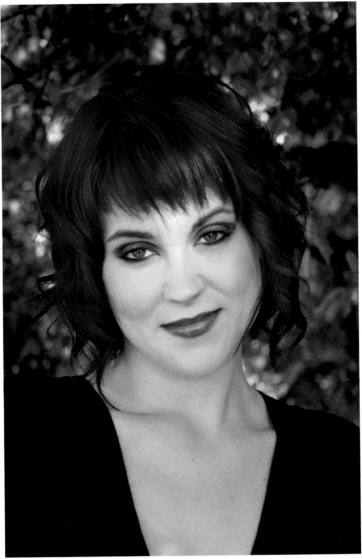

6.35 Rachel, South Congress, Austin, TX / Canon 30D with Canon EF 28-135mm f/3.5-5.6 IS, ISO 100, 1/200 sec. at f/5.6 with the 580EX set to E-TTL fired wirelessly via ST-E2 and shot through an umbrella for diffusion

Outdoor portrait photography practice

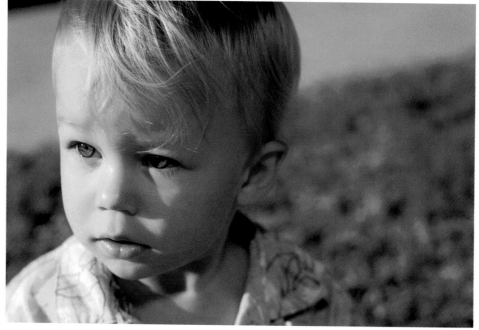

6.36 Caden, Elgin, TX / Canon 30D0 with Canon 28-135mm f/3.5-5.6 at 50mm, ISO 100, 1/1250 sec. at f/3.5 with the 430EX set to E-TTL with a Lightsphere for diffusion, evaluative metering

Table 6.10	
Taking Outdoor Portrait Pictures	
Setup	**Practice Picture:** Figure 6.36 was taken in November, using late afternoon light. Because the sun was setting, the color of the light was beautiful.
	On Your Own: When the sun gets lower in the sky toward late afternoon and evening, the sky reflects the warm color onto your subject. This time is often the best to take portraits outdoors.

Lighting

Practice Picture: I used the 430EX Speedlite to add some fill—because the sun was bright and low creating some fairly harsh shadows. The Speedlite was set to FP high-speed sync because of the sun's intensity, yet I wanted to use a wide aperture.

On Your Own: Use the fill flash setting whenever your subject is backlit or if the angle of the sun is creating harsh shadows.

Lens

Practice Picture: Canon EF 28-135mm f/3.5-5.6 IS set to 50mm.

On Your Own: Use a medium-to-long telephoto lens to flatten your model's features. The farther you are away from the model, the less the apparent distance from their features is. Remember that if you are using a wide-angle lens at close range, your subject may end up with distorted features, like a larger nose and smaller ears.

Camera Settings

Practice Picture: Aperture Priority setting, evaluative metering. I chose the AP setting in order to choose a wide aperture to throw the background out of focus. The light meter was set to evaluative in order to use the Speedlite to create a fill-flash.

On Your Own: Use Aperture Priority to be able to set your aperture to control your depth of field.

Exposure

Practice Picture: 1/1250 sec. at f/3.5, ISO 100.

On Your Own: Be sure you set your aperture so that your subject's entire face is in focus, but the background is out of focus so that the background isn't competing with your model for attention.

Accessories

I used a Lightsphere to diffuse the light from the flash. A reflector of some sort can also be used to fill in any deep shadows on your subject.

Outdoor portrait photography tips

✦ **Shoot early in the morning or late in the afternoon.** The sunlight when the sun is rising or setting can give your subjects a pleasing warm tone. When the sun is high in the sky during the mid-afternoon hours, the light is often harsh and can cause severe shadows.

✦ **Use a wide aperture.** Using a wide aperture creates a pleasing out-of-focus background. This effect is known as *bokeh*, pronounced *bo-keh*. This comes from the Japanese word "boke" which means fuzziness or dizziness.

Still Life and Product Photography

In still life and product photography, lighting is the key to making the image work. You can set a tone using creative lighting to convey the feeling of the subject. You can also use lighting to show texture, color, and form to turn a dull image into a great one.

When practicing for product shots or experimenting with a still life, the first task you need to undertake is to find something to photograph. It can be one object or a collection of objects. Remember if you are shooting a collection of objects, try to keep within a particular theme so the image has a feeling of continuity. Start by deciding which object you want to have as the main subject; then place the other objects around it, paying close attention to the balance of the composition.

The background is another important consideration when photographing products or still life scenes. Having an uncluttered background in order to showcase your subject is often best, although you may want to show the particular item in a scene. An example of this would be possibly photographing a piece of fruit on a cutting board with a knife in a kitchen.

Diffused lighting is essential in this type of photography. You don't want harsh shadows making your image look like it was shot with a flash. The idea is to light it so it doesn't look as if it were lit. You want to use an umbrella or softbox to soften the shadows. If none of these is available, bouncing the flash off of the ceiling or a nearby wall can do the trick.

Even with diffusion, the shadow areas need some filling in. You can do this by using a second Speedlite as fill or by using a fill card. A *fill card* is a piece of white foam board or poster board used to bounce some light from the main light back into the shadows lightening them a bit. When using two or more Speedlites, be sure that your fill light isn't too bright, or it can cause you to have two shadows. Remember, the key to good lighting is to emulate the natural lighting of the sun.

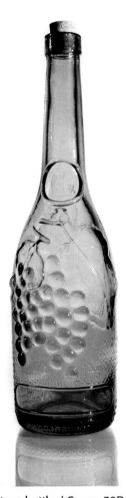

6.37 Vintage bottle / Canon 30D with Canon 38-135mm f/3.5-5.6 at 33mm, ISO 100, 1/60 sec. at f/4 with one 430EX and one 580EX in slave mode lighting the background fired with the ST-E2. All Speedlites set to Manual mode +3 FEC

Inspiration

When searching for subjects for a still life shot, try using some personal items. Objects such as jewelry or watches, a collection of trinkets you bought on vacation, or even seashells you brought home from the beach. If you're interested in cooking, try photographing some of the interesting dishes you can prepare. Fruits and vegetables are always good subjects, especially when they have vivid colors or interesting texture.

When photographing products, as opposed to a still life, it's essential to add some interest to the image. After all, product photography is all about marketing the item. There is a variety of ways this can be accomplished. Adding a splash of color by using gels, using selective focus to pull the viewer's attention to a certain part of the image, and focusing the light from the flash on a specific part of the product can help to add a little more diversity to the image. Sometimes adding a little action can go a long way, as in figure 6.33, where I used a splash to add some action in what would have been a static shot of a cup of liquid.

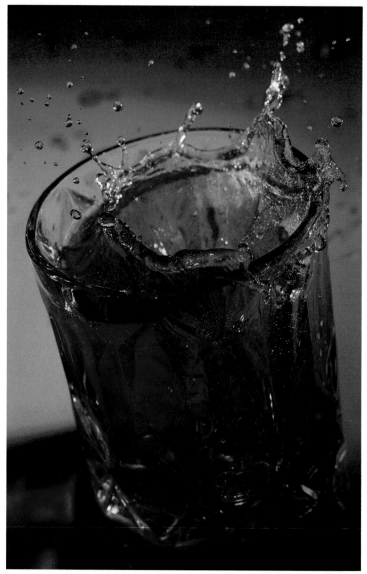

6.38 Splash / Canon 30D with Canon 50mm f/1.8, ISO 100, 1/60 sec. at f/8 with one 580EX set to E-TTL, evaluative mode, fired at 45° toward the backdrop

Still life and product photography practice

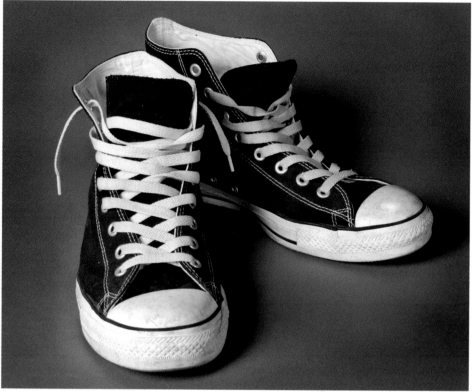

6.39 Favorite shoes / Canon 30D with Canon 18-55mm f/3.5-5.6 at 31mm, ISO 100, 1/60 sec. at f/10 with one 580EX and one 430EX set to slave mode fired with ST-E2 set to E-TTL Ratio 1:2

Table 6.11
Taking Still Life and Product Pictures

Setup	**Practice Picture:** For figure 6.39, I set up an old pair of favorite shoes on grey seamless paper.
	On Your Own: Keep your set simple, but still try to evoke a mood. Try to use a background that's complimentary for the color of the subject or subjects you are photographing.

Continued

Table 6.11 *(continued)*

Lighting	**Practice Picture:** For this shot I used one 430EX Speedlite and one 580EX. For the main light I had the 580EX in a softbox positioned up high. For the fill I placed a second Speedlite in a softbox fairly close up on the right side. I placed the fill light close in order to use the Speedlite to fill in the dark shadows created by the main light. **On Your Own:** Make sure your light is well diffused to soften the shadows. Take a lot of test shots to see how the light is showing off the texture of your subject.
Lens	**Practice Picture:** Canon 18-55mm f/3.5-5.6 at 31mm. **On Your Own:** Use a fairly wide angle lens. Using a wide-angle lens enables you to add an interesting perspective to the subject.
Camera Settings	**Practice Picture:** Manual mode. **On Your Own:** Manual mode or Aperture Priority mode to be able to control the depth of field.
Exposure	**Practice Picture:** 1/60 sec. at f/10, ISO 100. **On Your Own:** Because your subject is stationary, the shutter speed isn't as much of an issue. Be sure you set your aperture so you can carry enough depth of field to ensure that everything is in focus from front to back.
Accessories	Use a softbox or umbrella to diffuse the light from the Speedlites.

Still life and product photography tips

✦ **Keep it simple.** Don't try to pack too many objects in your composition. Having too many objects for the eye to focus on can lead to a confusing image.

✦ **Use items with bold colors and dynamic shapes.** Bright colors and shapes can be eye-catching and add interest to your composition.

✦ **Vary your light output.** When using more than one light on the subject, use one as a fill light, setting it to fire at a lower power in order to add a little depth to subject by creating subtle shadows.

Studio Portrait Photography

Shooting portraits in the studio involves more setup than other types of portrait photography. Whether your studio is in a set location or it's portable, the setup usually includes a background with stands, at least two lights with stands, umbrellas or softboxes, reflectors, and so forth.

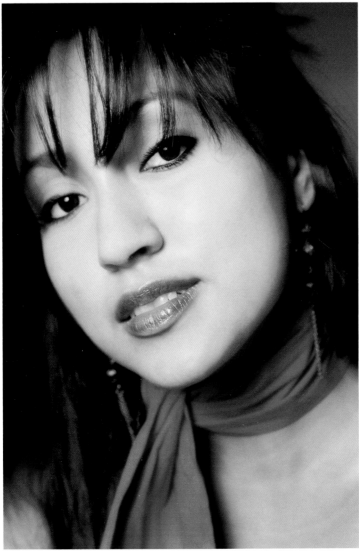

6.40 Inne, Dead Sailor Productions studio, Austin, TX / Canon 30D with Canon 50mm f/1.8, ISO 100, 1/60 sec at f/3.5, 580EX on stand high camera left fired through an umbrella; 430EX with red gel fired at background; ST-E2 set to E-TTL ratio 1:2

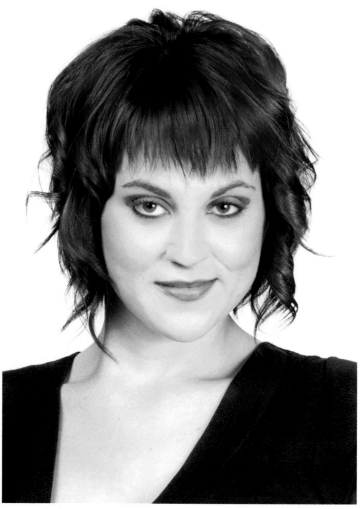

6.41 Rachel, Wet Salon, Austin TX / Canon 30D with Canon 55-200mm f/4.5-5.6 at 100mm, ISO 320, 1/250 sec. at f/9 with the 430EX and 580EX set to slave mode bounced from an umbrella, ST-E2 as master set to E-TTL Ratio 1:1, evaluative metering. Hair and makeup by Julia Czech.

Studio portraits are usually more formal than outdoor portraits, which tend to have a more relaxed feeling to them. Two major elements to remember when shooting a portrait in a studio are:

✦ **Control the background.** Being able to control your background keeps distracting elements out of your image and focuses the attention where it should be, on your subject.

✦ **Control the lighting.** Unlike when you're shooting outdoors, in the studio you choose where the light falls on your subject, how much light is falling on your subject, and how the shadows look, by using modifiers, such as umbrellas and softboxes.

Although studio portraits are more formal than outdoor portraits, don't be afraid to encourage your model to have fun with the shoot. You can try to make him or her laugh or suggest a few wacky poses. Also, remember that "formal" doesn't necessarily mean boring or serious. However, depending on your subject, you may find you like the more traditional, serious look.

As you do more and more portraits, you will find yourself developing a style. Almost all famous portrait photographers have their own personal style that reflects their own personality while also capturing the essence of the model.

Inspiration

When photographing studio portraits, I often have subjects go for a more glamorous look. It's a great feeling when subjects look at a portrait you took and they are completely impressed by how beautiful or handsome they look.

Outside of practicing on family and friends, to find models for these types of shots, a great place to start is at beauty salons. Hairstylists often need pictures for their portfolios and in exchange for the photography, will often find the models and do the hair and makeup for you.

Another good source of models are actors and models who are just starting out in the business. They are often willing to trade time for prints, better known as TFP or since the advent of digital, TFCD. It's a good way to get your portfolio built up without having to pay for models.

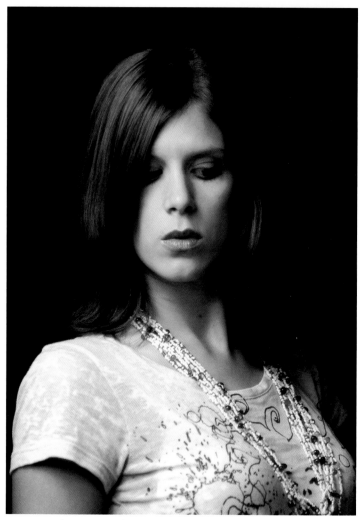

6.42 Beverly, Secret Hideout Studios, Austin TX / Canon 30D with Canon 55-200mm f/4.5-5.6 at 95mm, ISO 100, 1/60 sec. at f/5, with one 430EX controlled via ST-E2 set to E-TTL, evaluative metering

Studio portrait photography practice

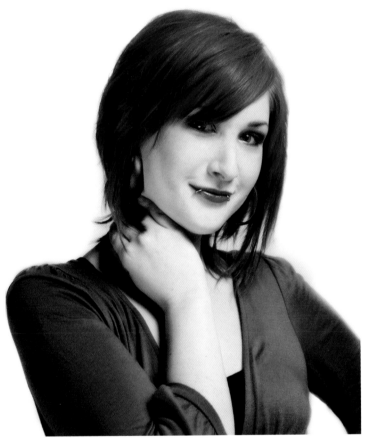

6.43 Rachel, Wet Salon, Austin TX / Canon 30D with Canon 55-200mm f/4.5-5.6 at 55mm, ISO 100, 1/160 sec. at f/4.5, with one 430EX bounced from an umbrella controlled via ST-E2 set to E-TTL, evaluative metering. Hair and makeup by Julia Czech.

Table 6.12
Taking Studio Portrait Pictures

Setup	**Practice Picture:** I set up my portable studio at Wet Salon in Austin TX to shoot some photographs. Figure 6.43 is just one of many I took that day.
	On Your Own: As long as you have a good background (and your equipment) you can do studio portraits anywhere.
Lighting	**Practice Picture:** I mounted one 430EX on a stand and placed it at a 60° angle high above the model. I also mounted an umbrella using a bracket and bounced the flash from the umbrella onto the model.
	On Your Own: Use one or more Speedlites to create the desired lighting pattern and mood.
Lens	**Practice Picture:** Canon 55-200mm f/4.5-5.6.
	On Your Own: Use a medium-to-long telephoto lens to enhance the model's features.
Camera Settings	**Practice Picture:** Manual mode.
	On Your Own: Use Manual or Aperture priority mode to control the depth of field.
Exposure	**Practice Picture:** 1/160 sec. at f/4.5, ISO 100.
	On Your Own: Set your shutter speed at or near your camera's sync speed. Using a wide aperture is not absolutely necessary when using a plain background, but it helps to let more light in so your Speedlite can fire at a lower power, giving you longer battery life.
Accessories	A fold-up reflector is a great idea. As you can see in figure 6.43, you can get professional-looking portraits using only one Speedlite on the model, but you need a reflector to bounce some light into the dark side of the face.

Studio portrait photography tips

✦ **Use a long lens.** Long lenses flatten your subject's features by reducing the apparent distance, which is the distance objects look from each other from a certain perspective. For example, if you use a wide-angle lens at close range it can cause the nose to look big while also causing the ears to look too small.

✦ **Use different color backgrounds.** Using colors that complement your subject's features and clothing can make a portrait stand out.

✦ **Focus on the eyes.** The most important part of a portrait is the eyes. Make sure that they are in focus. If the eyes are a little fuzzy, the whole portrait looks off.

✦ **Have a list of poses ready.** Subjects often feel uncomfortable posing unless they are professional models. By having poses in mind ahead of time, it minimizes setup changes and the shoot goes smoother.

✦ **Be ready.** As soon as your subject is relaxed and feels comfortable, the shooting becomes easier and poses become more natural.

✦ **Ask your model to bring some music.** Sometimes people feel more relaxed while listening to their favorite music.

Simple Posing for Great Portraits

CHAPTER

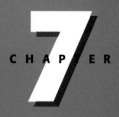

7

◆   ◆   ◆   ◆

In This Chapter

Posing basics

Refined posing techniques

Positions to avoid

Planning poses

◆   ◆   ◆   ◆

One of the most important aspects of portrait photography is knowing how to pose your subjects. If your model looks awkward or uncomfortable, your portrait isn't going to be a success. The key to a good portrait is having the model look natural.

To be a successful portrait photographer, you need to have good technical skills, but posing subjects is an art form unto itself. As soon as you start to master the art of posing subjects, you'll find that the quality of your work will grow by leaps and bounds.

Ultimately, you need to create a set of standards that you use that works best for the types of portraits you and your clients like to see. After you develop your own style, by sticking to your best practices, you will see great improvement in your portrait portfolio.

Posing Basics

Photographic posing isn't new; actually, posing has evolved over the centuries. Some of the best portraits I've ever seen weren't even photographs, but painted portraits dating back hundreds of years. In touring art museums here and abroad, I'm still amazed at the detail and subject matter of paintings created by masters of long ago. To be fair, portrait photography has taken the art form further, some say by leaps and bounds. A little combination of both styles goes a long way.

Whether it is classic or cutting-edge portraiture, some rules remain the same. Your subjects still need to seem natural and without any distortions to the person's features. You can follow a number of basic rules but don't have to adhere to them for every portrait. These rules are a great starting point for every digital portrait photographer.

Basic poses for individuals include:

✦ **Shoulders at an angle.** This is one of the first rules in portraiture. The subject's shoulders should be turned at an angle to your camera. Use this rule often, for both standing and seated situations. When the shoulders are evenly facing the photographer, the subject looks unnaturally wider. Figure 7.1 shows a simple portrait taken with the shoulders pointed at an angle to the camera. Try to ensure that the shoulder closer to the camera is lower than the other shoulder.

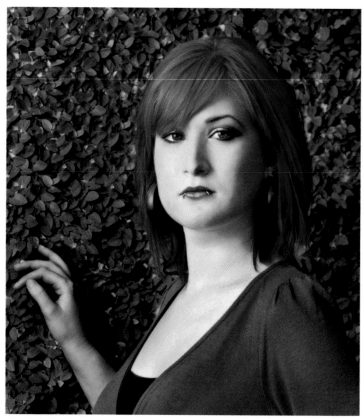

7.1 Pose your subjects with their shoulders pointed at an angle to the camera.

✦ **Head tilted.** After subjects turn their shoulders so they're on an angle, ask them to tilt and turn their head slightly so the head isn't in the same position as the shoulders. When you have your subjects tilt and turn their head slightly, you're also changing the position of the eyes, giving a more naturally interesting look to the portrait with a dynamic touch.

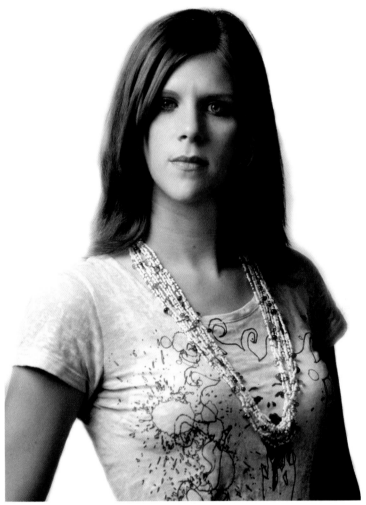

7.2 Even a very slight tilt of the head adds drama to a portrait.

Tip *When making changes to a person's posture, try not to make the changes dramatic. Usually, just a slight turn and tilt of the head does the trick. You don't want to have the pose appear overdone.*

✦ **Feet placed naturally.** If you're shooting full length portraits, whether the subject is standing or sitting, make sure you pay close attention to feet. You want the feet positioned close enough together, but not unnaturally. Additionally, if your subject is facing you on an angle, place the foot closest to you angled slightly more toward the camera than the other foot. This adds more balance to the subject in some portraits, and naturally turns the subject's body more toward the camera.

Tip *Try posing your subject's feet first and then work your way up.*

After you understand some of these basic posing techniques and try them out on occasion, you're ready for the next steps, which are more elaborate portrait posing techniques. I'm not talking about posing every single inch of a subject's body; just some subtle changes to posture or position can go a long way in making a great portrait.

Refined Posing Techniques

As a photographer, I consider posing an art form in itself. After I determine what type of portrait I'm photographing, I then go to work on setting up the entire body for the pose I want. I start with the feet and legs and then work my way up. Even though a small percentage of portraits are actually full-body length shots, a best practice is to pose the subject as if their entire body is going to be included in the portrait. While you are shooting, make sure to take a few full-length shots as you may discover a few hidden gems among your images that way.

Positioning the midsection

In the real world, not all of your subjects are going to be twenty-ish models that weigh 100 pounds. Mastering techniques where you can photographically slim the midsection of your subjects is important. This is increasingly important when photographing clients who are conscious of their weight.

Establish upfront with your subject whether they want full-length poses or just to be photographed from the waist up. To make subjects appear thinner, *never* have them pose square to the camera. For standing positions, have your subjects turn their hips toward the left or right, preferably away from the main light. You can also consider having your subjects shift their weight to the hip closest to the camera.

Other slimming techniques include:

✦ **Legs separated slightly.** In addition to having your subject turn his or her hips slightly to the left or right, you should also suggest a stance with the legs slightly separated. Avoid full-length portraits where both legs are positioned close together; keep a separation at the thighs when possible.

✦ **Legs crossed.** I use this pose quite often. Have your subject turn at an angle, either left or right (preferably toward the main light), and shift his or her weight to the leg closest to the camera with one leg crossing the other. This creates a slight lean that looks very natural in most cases.

7.3 Portrait showing the legs crossed, creating a slight lean, and one arm away from the body.

Clothing can also contribute to or hinder your efforts to illustrate a thinner appearance to your subject. Baggy clothing doesn't help. Be creative in those situations where your subject is wearing a pair of baggy pants, a baggy shirt, or a loose fitting dress. Have subjects lean a leg on a chair or lean on an object to thin out their appearance in the portrait when wearing baggy clothing.

Positioning the arms and hands

Working your way up, you can use a number of tips and techniques to properly position your subject's arms and hands. Using the body to make up the main composition, positioning of the arms and hands add to the desired look or style of the photograph. You want to make the person look his or her best.

Tips for positioning the shoulders, arms, and hands include:

✦ **Triangle pose.** If you're not shooting a full-length portrait, a common technique to properly frame the portrait is the triangular pose. Try filling the bottom of the frame with your subject's arms folded, filling in the bottom of the triangle, where the arms and shoulders lead up to the triangle's peak, the person's head.

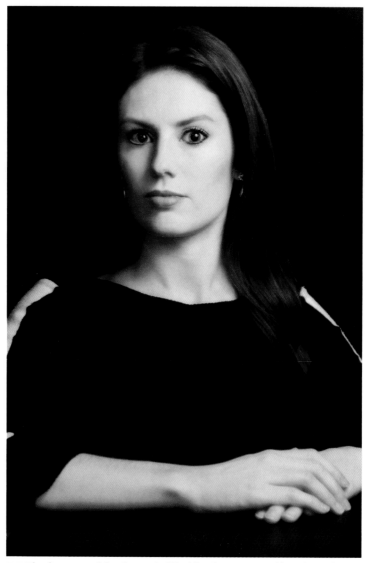

7.4 The bottom of the frame is filled by the arms and hands of the subject as placed in the triangle pose.

✦ **Shoulders diagonal.** Shoulders are going to be a major anchoring point for almost all of your poses. As a rule of thumb, your subject's shoulders should never be positioned horizontally across the frame. Have clients position their shoulders on a diagonal position to add interest to the portrait.

✦ **One arm away from the body.** To complete the body portion of your portrait, have the subject positioned with at least one arm away from his or her body to help define the midsection. Within this parameter, arms can be positioned in many ways. For waist-up portraits, having the arms leaning on a chair or other object gives a relaxed appearance to the portrait. Try having subjects shift their weight to their elbows and relax their forearms.

✦ **Hands relaxed.** Hands are often the most overlooked part of the body in portraits; however, paying attention to the detail when it comes to posing a subject adds to the quality of what you're trying to achieve. Hands are important, and you want to ensure that the subject isn't wearing any unusual bracelets or rings that can detract from your portrait. Be tactful and ask the subject if they can remove any distracting jewelry or accessory that may not work for the portrait. Additionally, make sure the subject's fingers are straightened and relaxed. You don't want fingers curled under in a portrait.

Note *There are exceptions to every rule. Always gauge what you ask of your subjects by their personalities and what you know about them. That pinky ring may be a family heirloom or that brooch a special gift. So, use your best judgment when setting up your portraits.*

Positioning the head and neck

The final step is positioning of the head. Simple adjustments, such as having the head tilted slightly or resting on an object, can add an artistic effect to any portrait. There are actually a few decisions to make when positioning the head, the first being what type of pose you and your subject want for the portrait.

For me, the eyes are the most important part of any portrait. Eye contact is a focal point where you need to ask your subjects to focus their gaze toward the camera. For some portraits, you want subjects to direct their eyes in another direction.

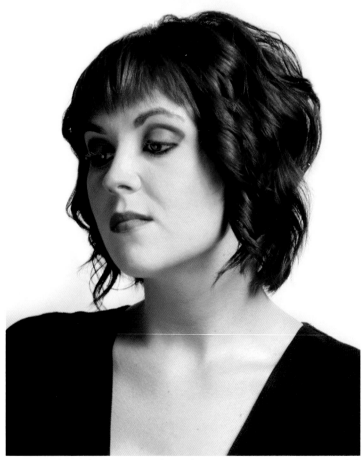

7.5 Sometimes, looking away from the camera can create a powerful portrait.

When taking portraits, I often have subjects try to focus their eyes in a few directions by first looking directly toward my lens, and then asking them look to the left, right, slightly up, or slightly down.

Tip *When shooting portraits either indoors or outdoors, consider adding fill flash to create a catch light in your subject's eyes. The eyes are an important component in your overall posing, and attention to detail, such as including catch light, adds to the quality of your portraits.*

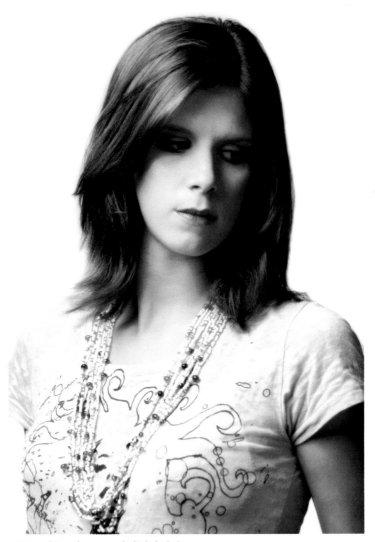

7.6 Looking down and slightly left

In addition to paying close attention to the eyes, other areas of the head are important as well. You already know about tilting the head, but a few more aspects you need to consider when posing your subjects are:

✦ **Hair.** For individuals with long hair, make sure you have enough room in your frame to showcase that part of the person

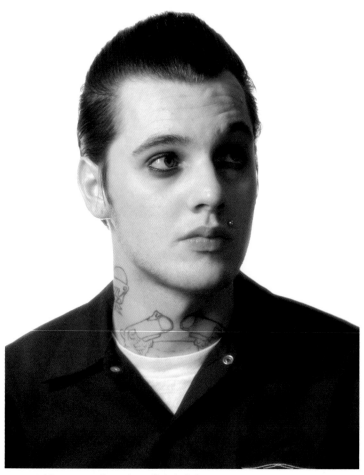

7.7 Looking up and turning slightly left

Tip

An often overlooked part of the portrait is the subject's neck. Necks often reflect weight or age of a subject. To achieve a pleasing portrait, you may consider either hiding portions of the neck with clothing, or positioning the portrait to reduce the amount of the person's neck

included in the portrait. While we're on the subject, a good technique to use to reduce double chins is to have your subject slightly tip their head upward.

Cross-Reference

For group portrait posing tips, see the section on group portraits in Chapter 6.

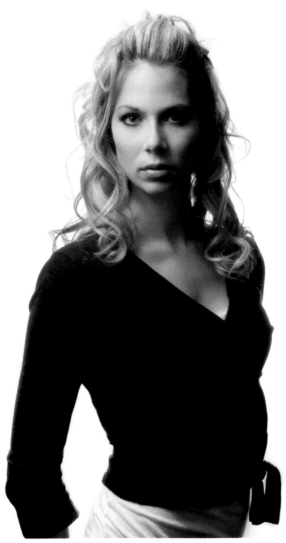

7.8 Pay close attention to hair and positioning the head to where the hair is a complementary part of the composition.

Positions to Avoid

When it comes to posing, there are a number of techniques to avoid, and even more techniques you need to take into consideration. A few techniques to *avoid* include:

✦ **Try not to use the typical yearbook pose excessively.** Unless you're shooting yearbook photos for a school or this is what your client wants, try to stay away from the typical head and shoulders shot. Be creative.

✦ **Straight in front of the camera poses.** This pose only works well for portraits where you want a plain look. Otherwise, the subject standing directly in front of the camera, looking straight at your digital camera is rather dull. Try to avoid poses where the person's posture is straight vertically (as in when the spine is in a perfect vertical line), or where the shoulders form a perfect horizontal line in the frame. These poses may be fine for snapshots, but not creative portraits.

✦ **The chin too low or too high.** Head positioning is very important. Make sure your portrait subject's chin isn't pointed too low to a point where the eyes aren't illuminated, and watch out for having the chin too high so that your model looks uncomfortable.

✦ **Don't instruct the person on how to pose.** Show them how it's done instead. When you demonstrate to the person how to pose, he or she understands your desires much more clearly. Direct your subjects by showing, not telling, and the shoot moves much quicker!

✦ **Negative body language.** The last thing your portrait subjects want to see is a scowl on your face when they make a pose you don't like. You want your subjects to have a good time having their portraits taken, so always remain upbeat, positive, and constructive in the words you say and the body language you communicate.

Have some fun with your subjects — keep in mind that a successful portrait session is dependent on your subject feeling comfortable and your creativity. If you're at ease, the person you are photographing is going to be more relaxed. Encourage your subject to act natural; ask them if it's okay for you to take photos of them when they are not necessarily posed. You may end up with some photos your subject really likes and even a few for your portfolio.

Planning Poses

Before you actually start working with your subject, first determining what type of portrait you want to create is best. Are you trying to shoot a casual, traditional, or a glamour type portrait? Obviously, if you're hired by your subject, you need to find out what the client's preferences are. You may even want to try mixing things up a bit, shooting some traditional poses, photojournalistic style poses, casual poses, glamour poses, or maybe all of them. The important aspect to remember is to talk to your subject and find out what his or her expectations are. Don't be afraid to make artistic suggestions — you're the photographer after all.

Casual portrait posing

A favorite type of posing is the type where you're capturing the subject just as he would be positioned in everyday life: playing the piano, watching TV, or lounging around home. The goal with casual posing is to capture the image of the subject as if there were no posing at all.

I find the best types of casual posing are when parts of the body are positioned to allude to relaxation, such as the head resting in the a hand, elbows resting on knees, the head resting on a wall or chair, or legs crossed when sitting. Any posture where the subject looks relaxed elicits a casual pose.

Traditional poses

Traditional posing is often referred to as "yearbook," or conservative, posing, but it does definitely have its place in the portrait world. Many publications use these types of portraits from school publications to corporate reports. As a photographer, you are often concentrating on artistic styling, but there are many portraits in which traditional posing is more desirable and where posing is performed in a subtle manner. A conservative or traditional portrait can be used as part of a wedding album or can even be used in a photojournalistic publication.

Traditional posing often includes these characteristics:

✦ **Conservative expressions.** Slight smiles, but not laughing is the key with traditional posing. For business publications, subjects often have more serious facial expressions.

✦ **Plain backgrounds.** For traditional portraits, plain backgrounds of a solid color, dyed, or painted muslin are commonly used.

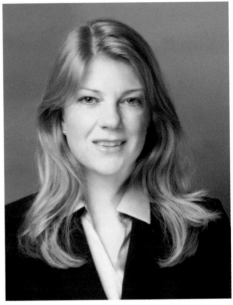

7.9 Traditional portraits are used for purposes ranging from personal portraits to photojournalistic publications.

✦ **Seated position.** Often photographers forget that people can look perfectly natural in a seated position in some cases.

✦ **Standing position.** Having subjects standing while taking traditional portraits is commonly a best practice, as the subjects are often dressed conservatively, in a suit or other more formal attire, and standing can make them feel more comfortable.

Photojournalistic poses

Photojournalists tend to take portraits while their subjects are in the midst of doing what they normally do or while they are engaged in some sort of activity. It's easier to capture someone's personality while they're taking part in some activity that they enjoy. These types of portraits are similar in feel to a casual portrait, but they are even more relaxed.

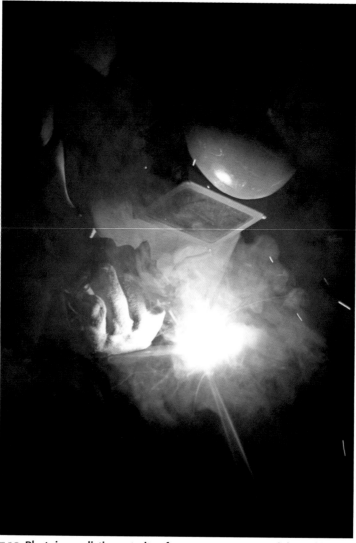

7.10 Photojournalistic portraits often convey a sense of the subject's personality.

Photojournalistic poses are much less constricting than traditional posing. In other words, you and your subject can have some fun coming up with interesting poses. However, with photojournalistic style photography, you really don't have to pose your subjects at all. Just let them do their thing and capture their images as they would be in their natural environment. This type of portraiture is more commonly known as an environmental portrait.

 For more on environmental portraits, see Chapter 6.

Photojournalistic style posing has become increasingly popular in wedding photography in the past few years, and I attribute that to the advent of digital photography.

Wedding photographers traditionally used standard, conservative poses; however, in the past few years, a crop of new, adventurous photographers using photojournalism techniques in their wedding work have emerged, slowly replacing the traditional posed wedding photography.

When engaged in a photojournalistic photo session, asking the client up front what his or her expectations are is best. Ask your clients to describe the types of portraits they would prefer. This information helps you request certain behavior of your clients when you're taking their portraits.

Glamour style

Glamour posing is what you expect to see on the cover of a trendy or fashion magazine or in the fashion pages within a magazine. Simply put, glamour photography is supposed to be sexy. I'm not referring to nude images; you can accomplish a sensual photograph without showing a lot of skin or any skin at all.

Naturally, glamour photographs are used capturing images to either appeal to the opposite sex or to be used in magazines or other types of printed material to evoke a feeling of sexiness that compels consumers to buy. Just flip through a popular catalog or a popular magazine aimed specifically at women or men, and the pages are filled with images of attractive people in sensuous poses, catering to the reader. Glamour photography is most popular in these types of media.

In addition to glamour photographs used in magazines or advertising, there is also a very large following of glamour photography as an art form. Artistically, the human form is a favorite subject for many photographers and art collectors. Creative possibilities are endless with so many different types of faces in the world from which to choose. The advent of digital photography and the Web has helped bring this art form to an entire new level, allowing millions to easily view images normally limited to art galleries or fine art photography books.

For the digital portrait photographer, thinking of glamour photography as an art form is important. When shooting glamour photographs in the studio, being professional at all times is extremely important. Make sure your models are comfortable with the types of poses they are expected to assume and invite them to participate in creating the poses.

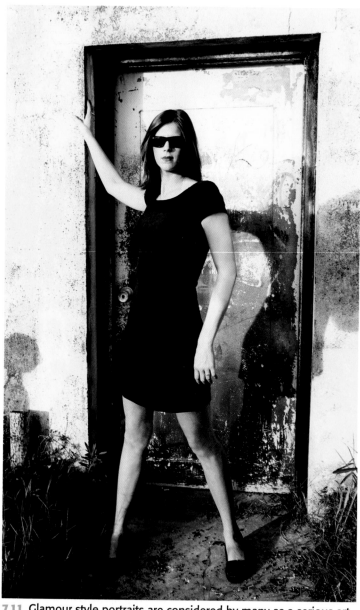

7.11 Glamour style portraits are considered by many as a serious art form.

Appendixes

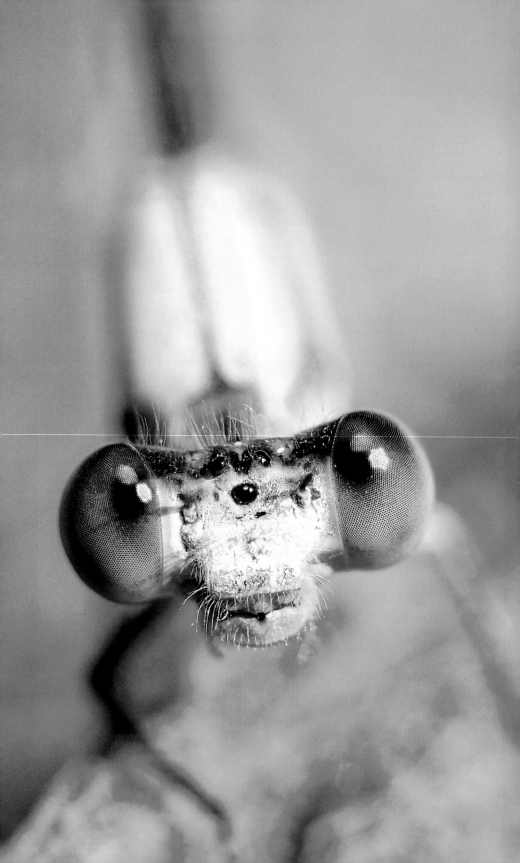

Basic Rules of Composition

 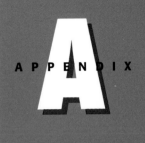

Photography, as with any other art form, has its general rules. Although they are called rules, they are really nothing more than useful guidelines. Although some photographers—notably Ansel Adams, who was quoted as saying "The so-called rules of photographic composition are, in my opinion, invalid, irrelevant and immaterial,"—claim to have eschewed the rules of composition, when you look at many of these photographer's photos (including Adams'), their photographs follow the rules perfectly.

This isn't to say you need to follow every one of the rules every time you take a photograph. As I said, these are really just general guidelines, that when followed, can make your images more powerful and interesting.

Another famous photographer, Edward Weston, said that "Consulting the rules of composition before taking a photograph, is like consulting the laws of gravity before going for a walk." Again, when you look at his photographs, they tend to follow the rules.

When you're starting out in photography, it is a good idea to pay attention to the rules of composition. Eventually, however, you become so accustomed to following the guidelines that it becomes second nature and you no longer need to consciously consult the rules of composition; you just inherently follow them.

Keep It Simple

Simplicity. This is arguably the most important rule in creating a good image. You want the subject of your photograph to be immediately recognizable. When you have too many competing elements in your image it can be difficult for the viewer to decide what to focus on.

Another element to consider is the background. Many times the background information isn't necessary to complete the image. Open up your aperture and let the background go out of focus so it isn't drawing attention away from your subject.

Changing your perspective to the subject can sometimes be all you need to do in order to remove a distracting element from your image. Walk around and try to shoot from different angles.

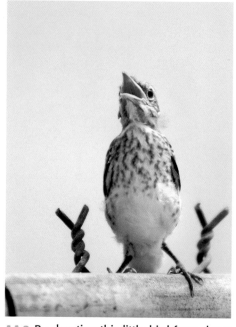

AA.2 By shooting this little bird from down low, you would never know that there was a busy racetrack just behind him.

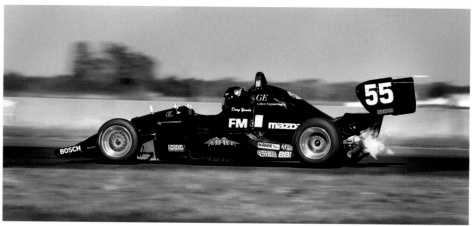

AA.1 There's no guessing what the subject in this photograph is.

The Rule of Thirds

Most of the time you are probably tempted to take the main subject of your photograph and stick it smack dab in the middle of the frame. This makes sense and most of the time works pretty well for snapshots. To create more interesting and dynamic images oftentimes it works better to put the main subject of the image a little off-center.

The Rule of Thirds is a compositional rule that has been in use for many hundreds of years. With the Rule of Thirds you divide the image into nine equal parts using two equally spaced horizontal and vertical lines, kind of like a tic-tac-toe pattern. You want to place the main subject of the image where one of these lines intersects, as illustrated in figure AA.3. The subject doesn't necessarily have to be right on the intersection of the line, but merely being close to it is enough to take advantage of the Rule of Thirds.

Another way to use the Rule of Thirds is to place the subject in the center of the frame, but at the bottom or top third of the frame as illustrated in figure AA.4. This part of the rule is especially useful when photographing landscapes. You can place the horizon at or near the top or bottom line, but you almost never want to place it in the middle. Notice in figure AA.5, the mountain range is covering the bottom third of the entire frame.

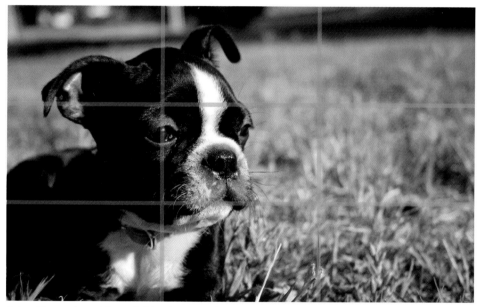

AA.3 The main subject of this photograph, Henrietta, is placed in one of the intersecting lines according to the Rule of Thirds.

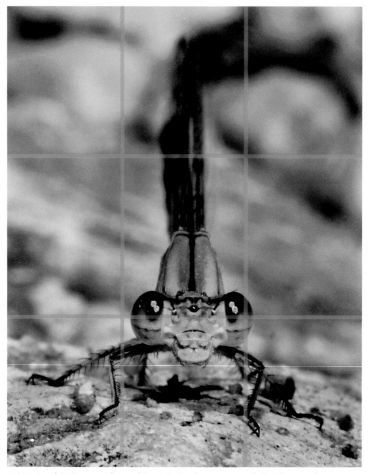

AA.4 In this image the subject is in the center of the frame, but at the bottom third.

When using the Rule of Thirds, keep in mind the movement of the subject. If the subject is moving you want to be sure to keep most of the frame in front of the subject so it doesn't look like it's going to fly right off of the picture. You want to keep the illusion that the subject has someplace to go.

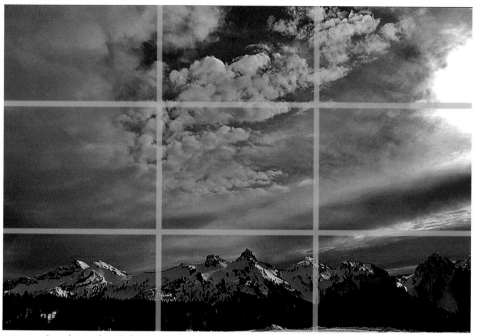

AA.5 Using the Rule of Thirds in a landscape

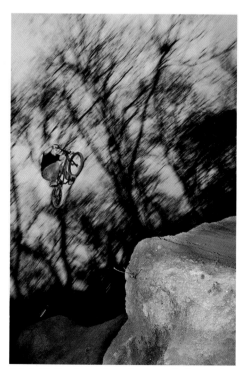

> **Tip**
>
> *Remember that there are exceptions to every rule, including the Rule of Thirds.*

The Rule of Thirds is a very simple guideline, but can work wonders in making your images more interesting and visually appealing. After you use this several times, you'll start composing to the Rule of Thirds without even realizing it.

AA.6 Notice how there is space in front of Pants, the BMX rider, giving the viewer the visual impression of where he is going to land.

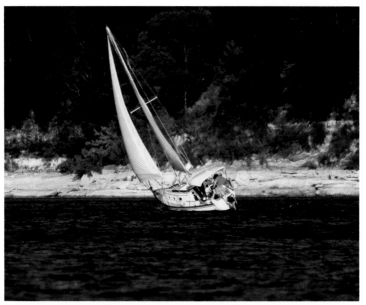

AA.7 Placing the sailboat directly in the middle results in an okay snapshot.

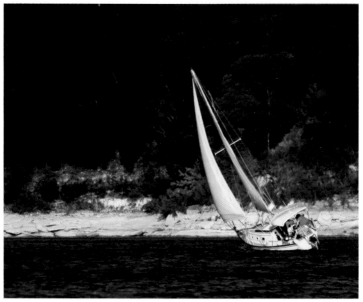

AA.8 Recomposing to place the sailboat in the lower-right third of the frame results in a much more dramatic image.

Leading Lines and S-Curves

Another good way to add drama to an image is to use a *leading line* to draw the viewer's eye through the picture. A leading line is an element in a composition that leads the viewer's eye toward the subject. A leading line can be a road, sidewalk, railroad tracks, buildings, columns, or a million other things.

In general, you want your leading line to go in a specific direction. Most commonly, a leading line leads the eye from one corner of the picture to another. A good rule of thumb to follow is to have your line stretching from the bottom-left corner leading toward the top-right corner.

You can also use leading lines to go from the bottom of the image to the top and vice-versa. Depending on the subject matter, this can work equally as well. For the most part, leading lines heading in this direction lead to a *vanishing point*. A vanishing point is the point at which parallel lines converge and seem to disappear. Figure AA.9 shows a leading line ending in a vanishing point. Keep in mind, when using one rule you may have to break another. For example, figure AA.9 has the horizon in the center in order to better call attention to the leading lines of the railroad tracks.

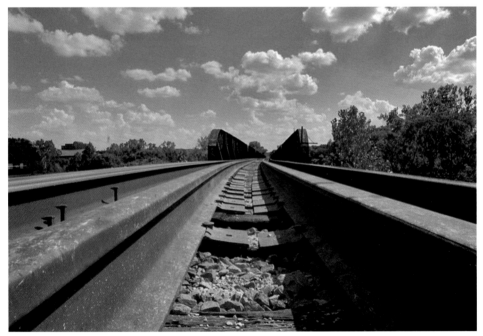

AA.9 A leading line ending in a vanishing point.

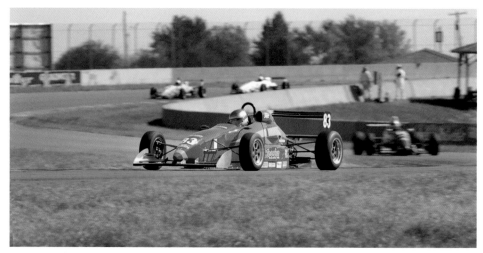

AA.10 In this image, the racetrack and the barrier together form an S-curve that draws the eye through the whole image.

Another nice way to use a leading line is with an *S-curve*. An S-curve is exactly what it sounds like; it resembles the letter S. An S-curve can go from left to right or right to left. The S-curve draws the viewer's eye up from the bottom of the image through the middle, on to the corner and back to the other side again.

Helpful Hints

Along with the major rules, here are several other helpful guidelines.

✦ **Frame the subject.** Use elements of the foreground to make a frame around the subject to keep the viewer's eye from wandering.

✦ **Avoid having the subject looking directly out of the frame.** Having the subject looking out of the photograph can be distracting to the viewer. Keep the subject facing what's in the frame, not what's outside of it.

✦ **Avoid mergers.** A *merger* is when an element from the background appears to a part of the subject. Like the snapshot of your granny at the park where it looks like she has a tree growing out of the top of her head.

✦ **Try not to cut through the joint of a limb.** When composing or cropping your picture, it's best not to end the frame on a joint, such as an elbow or a knee cap. This can be psychologically disturbing to the viewer.

✦ **Avoid having bright spots or unnecessary details near the edge.** Having anything bright or detailed near the edge of the frame draws the viewer's eye away from the subject and out of the image.

✦ **Avoid placing the horizon or strong horizontal or vertical lines in the center of the composition.** This cuts the image in half and makes it hard for the viewer to decide which half of the image is important.

✦ **Separate the subject from the background.** Make sure the background doesn't have similar colors or textures as the subject. If necessary, try shooting from different angles or use a shallow depth-of-field to achieve separation.

✦ **Fill the frame.** Try to make the subject the most dominant part of the image. Avoid having lots of empty space around the subject, unless it enhances the composition.

✦ **Use odd numbers.** When photographing multiple subjects odd numbers seem to work best.

These are just a few of the probably hundreds of composition guidelines out there. And remember, these are not hard and fast rules, just simple pointers that can help you on your way to creating interesting and amazing images.

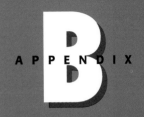

Resources

There is a lot valuable information available on the Internet for photographers. This appendix is a resource to help you discover some of the many ways to learn more about the Canon Speedlite System and about photography in general.

Informational Web Sites

With the amount of information on the Web, sometimes it is difficult to know where to look or where to begin. These are a few sites that I suggest you start with when looking for reliable information about your Canon Speedlites or photography in general.

Canon

When you want to access the technical specifications for Canon Speedlites, cameras, or lenses visit the Canon Web site `http://usa.canon.com`.

Strobist.com

This site has lots of tips and tutorials on how to effectively use shoe-mounted flashes on and off camera. It's loaded with tips and DIY projects for making modifiers for your flash. `http://www.strobist.blogspot.com/`

Photo.net

The Photo.net site, at `http://photo.net`, is a large site containing resources from equipment reviews, to forums on a variety of topics, to tutorials, and more. If you are looking for specific photography-related information and aren't sure where to look, this is a great place to start.

Photocritic.org

The do-it-yourself blog found at www.photo critic.org, is an informative site that contains topics ranging from the science of red eye to great tips and ideas on how to get better results from a variety of equipment. It is a community-type site with contests, polls, and even some interesting project suggestions.

Workshops

There are a multitude of different workshops that offer training for photographers. Here is a list of some of the different workshops that are available to you.

Anderson Ranch Arts Center

www.andersonranch.org

Ansel Adams Gallery and Workshops

ww.anseladams.com

Brooks Institute Weekend Workshops

http://workshops.brooks.edu

Mentor Series

www.mentorseries.com

Palm Beach Photographic Centre Workshops

www.workshop.org

Missouri Photo Workshop

www.mophotoworkshop.org

Mountain Workshops

www.mountainworkshops.org

Photography at the Summit

www.photographyatthesummit.com

The Workshops

www.theworkshops.com

Rocky Mountain Photo Adventures

www.rockymountainphotoadventures.com

Santa Fe Workshops

www.santafeworkshops.com

Online Photography Magazines and Other

Some photography magazines also have Web sites that offer photography articles and often information that isn't even found in the pages of the magazine. The following is a list of a few photography magazines' Web sites as well as some other photo-related sites where you may find useful content.

Communication Arts

www.commarts.com/CA/

Digital Photographer

http://digiphotomag.com

Digital Photo Pro

www.digitalphotopro.com

Flickr

www.flickr.com

Ken Rockwell

www.kenrockwell.com

Outdoor Photographer

www.outdoorphotographer.com

Photo District News

www.pdnonline.com

Popular Photography & Imaging

www.popphoto.com

Shutterbug

www.shutterbug.net

Glossary

AE (Auto-Exposure) A general purpose shooting mode where the camera selects the aperture and shutter speed using its metered reading. On some cameras, the ISO settings are automatically set also.

AE/AF lock A camera setting that lets you lock the current exposure and/or autofocus setting prior to taking a photo. This button lets you recompose without holding the shutter release button halfway down.

AF assist illuminator In low light and low contrast shooting conditions, the AF (autofocus) assist illuminator automatically emits a light. It is located in the front bottom of the flash. The AF-assist beam is compatible with most recent Canon cameras, helping the camera to focus properly.

aperture Also referred to as the f-stop setting of the lens. The aperture controls the amount of light allowed to enter through the camera lens. The higher the f-stop numerical setting, the smaller the aperture is opened on the lens. Wider f-stop settings are represented by lower numbers, such as f/2. The wider the aperture, the less depth-of-field in the image. The smaller the aperture, the more depth-of-field you have, and more of the background will be in focus in the image.

aperture priority A camera setting where you choose the aperture, and the camera automatically adjusts the shutter speed according to the camera's metered readings. Aperture priority is often used by the photographer to control depth-of-field.

autofocus The ability of the camera to obtain and maintain accurate focus of the subject.

bounce flash Pointing the flash head in an upward position or toward a wall, thus softening the light illuminated off the subject. Bouncing the light often eliminates shadows and provides a smoother light for portraits.

catchlight Using the 580EX catchlight panel while pointing the flash head straight up provides the light needed to highlight a portrait subject's eyes and a small amount of fill flash.

channel Also referred to as *communication channel*. To avoid interfering with other wireless flash users in the same vicinity, the master and slave units can communicate on one of four channels. Communications in Speedlite System are partially based on setting the master and all additional Speedlites to the same channel. If by chance another photographer is using the same channel in the vicinity, your Speedlite System units may fire from the other photographer's control. To avoid this, set the master and other Speedlites to a different channel.

close-up flash Another term for using flash when doing macro photography.

colored gel filters Colored translucent filters, usually made from a form of polycarbonite, that fit over the flash head, changing the color of the light emitted on the subject. You use colored gels to create a colored hue of an image. Gels are often used to change the color of a white background when shooting portraits or still life photos, by placing the gel over the flash head and firing the flash at the background. The name "gels" stems from the early form of filters used in theatres, which were typically made from gelatin.

compatibility The ability of a camera, lens, or Speedlite to operate correctly when connected to one another. For example, to take advantage of all wireless lighting capabilities, the Speedlite, digital SLR, and lenses must be compatible.

continuous flash The ability to use a camera's continuous shooting modes with a Speedlite and have the Speedlite fire correctly adjusted flashes with each exposure.

contacts Electronic contacts located on the bottom of a Speedlite's shoe that makes contact with the camera's hot shoe, thus electronically connecting the Speedlite to the camera.

Canon EOS Speedlite System Also referred to as Speedlite System, allows for multiple flash capabilities in a wireless environment, taking advantage of communication of exposure information between the camera, master flash unit, and remote Speedlites. Canon's wireless lighting system utilizes compatible SLRs, E-TTL metering, the 580EX, 430EX, ST-E2 Commander, the MT-24EX macro twin light, and the MR-14EX macro ring light.

custom functions and settings The ability to customize Speedlite features and settings. Custom functions and settings can be made on both the Speedlite(s) and the camera, depending on the functionality desired.

default settings Factory settings of the Speedlite. When connecting your Speedlite to your camera, the Speedlite works automatically while in auto, aperture, shutter priority, or program modes.

depth of field The distance in front of and behind the subject that appears to be in focus.

digital SLR Single lens reflex camera with interchangeable lenses and an image sensor.

E-TTL mode Stands for evaluative through-the-lens. This metering mode allows for automatic flash output calculated by the camera's ability to communicate flash output levels to the Speedlite per the cameras metered reading.

E-TTL II Canon's newest and most advanced evaluative metering system for Speedlites. The E-TTL II metering system uses preflashes to help determine proper flash exposure.

exposure compensation The ability to take correctly exposed images by letting you adjust the exposure, typically in 1/3 stops from the metered reading of the camera. Enables the photographer to make manual adjustments to achieve desired results.

exposure mode Camera settings that let the photographer take photos in a variety of modes. When set to aperture priority, the shutter speed is automatically set according to the chosen aperture (f-stop) setting. In shutter priority mode, the aperture is automatically set according to the chosen shutter speed. When using manual mode, both aperture and shutter speeds are set by the photographer, bypassing the cameras metered reading. When using automatic mode, the camera selects the aperture and shutter speed. See also *scene mode*.

f-stop See *aperture*.

fill flash A lighting technique where the Speedlite provides enough light to illuminate the subject in order to eliminate shadows. Using a flash for outdoor portraits often brightens up the subject in conditions where the camera's meters light from a broader scene.

flash An external light source that produces an almost instant flash of light in order to illuminate a scene. Your Canon Speedlite is a flash.

flash exposure bracketing Taking a series of exposures while adjusting the flash exposure compensation up and/or down to ensure capturing the correct exposure.

flash exposure compensation Adjusting the flash output by +/- 3 stops in 1/3 stop increments. If images are too dark (underexposed), use flash exposure compensation to increase the flash output. If images are too bright (overexposed), you can use flash exposure compensation to reduce the flash output.

flash button A button on the rear panel of the Speedlite used to test fire the flash.

flash color information communication Color temperature information is automatically transmitted to the camera, providing the camera the correct white balance setting, giving you accurate color in your image when shooting photos with a Speedlite.

flash head The part of the Speedlite that houses the flash tube that fires when taking a flash photo. Flash heads can be adjusted for position. See also *flash head tilting*.

flash head tilting Adjusting the flash head horizontally or vertically by pressing the tilting/rotating lock release button and repositioning the flash head. Often used to point the flash in an upward position, such as when using bounce flash. Tilt the flash head straight up toward the ceiling when using the catch light panel.

flash head rotating lock release Buttons located on the left and right side of the flash head that when pressed, enable you to adjust the position of the flash head horizontally or vertically.

flash mode The method the flash uses to determine flash exposure. Flash modes include Auto Aperture, non-TTL automatic mode, and manual mode.

flash output level The output level of the flash as determined by one of the flash modes used. If using Manual mode, proper guide numbers need to be calculated in order to provide the correct amount of illumination.

flash shooting distance and range The actual range that the Speedlite has the ability to properly illuminate a subject. The range, typically between 2 to 60 feet, is dependent on the ISO sensitivity, aperture setting, and zoom head position.

flash sync mode Set in conjunction with camera settings, you can take flash photos in either front-curtain or rear-curtain sync. For most flash photos, the default is front-curtain sync. When using front-curtain sync, the flash fires right after the shutter opens completely. In rear-curtain sync, the flash fires just before the shutter begins to close.

Use rear-curtain sync in low light situations to avoid unnatural looking photos that occur due to subject movement.

FE lock The FE lock allows you to meter the subject to obtain the correct flash exposure and then lock the settings by pressing the FE lock button. You can then recompose the shot, usually with the subject to one side or the other, and take the photograph with the camera not metering for the new composition, thus retaining the proper flash exposure for the subject.

group When using wireless flash, Speedlites can be arranged in groups, where each group shares the same flash output setting controlled by the master flash unit.

guide number Indicates the amount of light emitted from the flash (at full power). Each model Speedlite has its own guide number, indicating the Speedlite's flash capability based on its maximum capability. The guide number is calculated based on an ISO setting, flash head zoom position, and distance to the subject.

high speed sync This feature allows you to shoot with flash up to the maximum shutter speed of the camera. This is achieved by causing the flash to emit a series of lower-powered flashes as the shutter opens along the digital sensor plane, rather than one flash as the shutter is completely open. When the high speed sync mode is not engaged the camera does not allow you to set the shutter speed to faster than the camera's rated sync speed. High-end flashes such as the 580EX and the 430EX have this feature. See also *sync speed*.

hot shoe Slot located on the top of the camera where the Speedlite connects. The hot shoe is considered "hot" because of its electronic contacts that allow communication between the Speedlite and the camera.

hot spot An overly bright spot on the subject caused by excessive or uneven lighting.

ISO sensitivity The ISO (International Standards Organization) setting on the camera indicates the light sensitivity setting. Film cameras need to be set to the film ISO speed being used (such as ISO 100, 200, or 400 film), where digital cameras ISO setting can be set to any available setting. In digital cameras, lower ISO settings provide better-quality images with less image noise, however the lower the ISO setting, the more exposure time is needed.

leading line An element in a composition that leads the viewer's eye toward the subject. See also *s-curve.*

lighting ratio This ratio is used to describe the difference in brightness between two light sources. A 1:1 ratio means both light sources are equal. A 1:2 ratio denotes that the second light is half as bright as the first, a 1:4 ratio describes the second light as being one-fourth as bright as the first, and so on.

manual exposure Bypassing the camera's internal light meter settings in favor of setting the shutter and aperture manually. Manual exposure is beneficial in difficult lighting situations where the camera's meter does not provide correct results. Switching to manual settings could entail a

"trial and error" process until the correct exposure is reviewed on the digital cameras LCD after a series of photos are taken. When using film cameras, there is no capability of reviewing images after they are taken.

manual mode Manually setting the flash output of the Speedlite independently from the calculated exposure of the camera.

master When using multiple Speedlites in a wireless flash configuration, the master flash unit is the one mounted on the camera. It controls the flash output of all remote units. The built-in Speedlites of some camera models can also act as a master flash. The master flash unit is also sometimes called a commander. See also *slave.*

merger An element in an image that looks as if it is part of the subject, although it doesn't belong, such as a plant that appears to be growing from a subject's shoulder.

metering Measuring the amount of light utilizing the camera's internal light meter. For most flash uses, Speedlites emit a pre-flash for the camera's light meter in order to achieve a properly exposed photo.

minimum recycling time The shortest amount of time a Speedlite needs to be able to properly fire a flash after a previous flash was fired. Speedlites are powered by batteries, and the minimum recycling time is a specification used to indicate how long it takes your Speedlite to recharge between photos.

Mode button The button on the Speedlite that changes the setting for an operation.

modeling light A secondary light, usually tungsten or halogen, built in to a studio strobe in order to visualize what the flash will look like. Canon's EX series Speedlites have a modeling "flash" that fires a short burst of rapid flashes that allow you to see the effect of the flash on the subject.

mounting foot locking wheel The wheel located on the bottom of the Speedlite hot shoe, that when turned, locks or unlocks the Speedlite from the camera's hot shoe.

multiple flash Using multiple Speedlites, wired or wirelessly in conjunction to illuminate a subject. Allows the photographer to create natural-looking photographs by creatively placing multiple flashes in different positions (and flash output) to achieve the desired lighting results.

Canon autofocus Speedlite Refers to any Canon model Speedlite that automatically adjusts the zoom range to match the focal length of the lens.

non-CPU lenses Older lenses that do not communicate electronically with the camera.

On/Off button The button located on the rear panel of the Speedlite that when turned on, powers up the Speedlite.

pilot light Located on the rear panel of the Speedlite, the pilot light indicates that the flash is ready to fire.

power zoom function When using compatible cameras and Speedlites, the ability for the Speedlites flash head to automatically zoom to the focused subject.

Programmed auto (P) When using a Speedlite with a compatible camera set to Programmed auto, the shutter speed is automatically set to the camera's sync shutter speed when using flash. On the camera, the shutter speed and aperture are automatically made when the subject is focused.

rear-curtain sync Setting the Canon camera to rear-curtain sync causes the flash to fire right before the shutter closes.

red-eye reduction A flash mode controlled by a camera setting that is used to prevent the subject's eyes from appearing red in color. The Speedlite fires multiple flashes just before the shutter is opened. As a general rule, the further the flash head is located from the axis of the camera lens, the less chance of getting the red-eye effect. You can combine red-eye reduction with slow-sync in low light situations.

remote See *slave*.

scene mode Available on some cameras, these are automatic modes in which the settings are adjusted to pre-determined parameters, such as a wide aperture for the portrait scene mode and high shutter speed for sports scene mode. See also *exposure mode*.

s-curve A leading that is shaped like the letter S. See also *leading line*.

shutter-priority In this camera mode, you set the desired shutter speed, and the camera automatically sets the aperture setting for you. Best used when shooting action shots to freeze motion of the subject using fast shutter speeds.

shutter speed The length of time the shutter is open to allow light to fall onto the imaging sensor. The shutter speed is measured in seconds or more commonly, fractions of seconds.

slave A Speedlite used in a multiple flash configuration that is not attached to the camera. The Speedlite attached to the camera is called a master, where all the other Speedlites are referred to as remotes, or slaves. See also *master*.

speedring A device used to attach a strobe to a softbox.

standby function The Speedlite's ability to automatically switch to a sleep mode if the Speedlite is not used for a predetermined period of time. The standby function prevents a rapid degradation of the Speedlites batteries. You can return the Speedlite to normal ready mode by pressing the shutter button half-way on the camera.

stroboscopic flash This is a flash mode on the 580EX which fires multiple flashes with which to capture multiple images of a moving subject in a single photographic frame.

sync speed Most flashes are limited to only being able to be used up to a certain shutter speed. This top speed is called the sync speed. The camera and the type of shutter mechanism being used limit the sync speed. See also *high speed sync*.

underexposure value The amount of underexposure set on the Speedlite (using exposure compensation) and indicated on the Speedlite's LCD panel.

vanishing point The point at which parallel lines converge and seem to disappear.

white balance Use white balance to compensate for the differences in color temperature common in different light sources. For example, a typical tungsten light bulb is very yellow-orange, so when adjusted properly, the camera's white balance setting adds blue to the image to ensure that the light looks like standard white light.

wireless remote flash unit See *slave*.

zoom head Also referred to as the Speedlite's flash head that has the capability of automatically moving the flash tube forward or backward during automatic flash operations to match the focal length of the lens being used.

Index

Continued

Continued

Continued

Continued

Pack the essentials.

These aren't just books. They're *gear*. Pack these colorful how-to guides in your bag along with your camera, iPod, and notebook, and you'll have the essential tips and techniques you'll need while on the go!

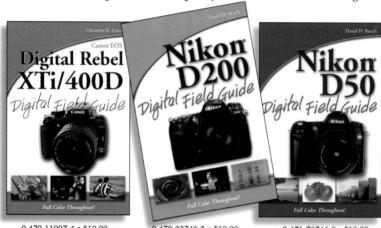

0-470-11007-4 • $19.99	0-470-03748-2 • $19.99	0-471-78746-9 • $19.99
978-0-470-11007-2	978-0-470-03748-5	978-0-471-78746-4

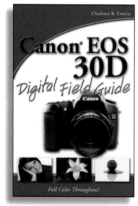 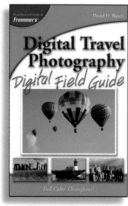 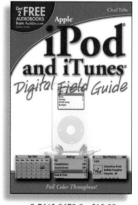

0-470-05340-2 • $19.99	0-471-79834-7 • $19.99	0-7645-9679-9 • $19.99
978-0-470-05340-9	978-0-471-79834-7	978-0-7645-9679-7

Also available

PowerBook and iBook Digital Field Guide • 0-7645-9680-2 • $19.99
Digital Photography Digital Field Guide • 0-7645-9785-X • $19.99
Nikon D70 Digital Field Guide • 0-7645-9678-0 • $19.99
Canon EOS Digital Rebel Digital Field Guide • 0-7645-8813-3 • $19.99

Available wherever books are sold

Wiley and the Wiley logo are registered trademarks of John Wiley & Sons, Inc. and/
or its affiliates. All other trademarks are the property of their respective owners.

WILEY
Now you know.
wiley.com